WHAT PEOPLE ARE SAYING ABOUT
It's Your Kid, Not a Gerbil

"Dr. Kevin Leman is the go-to guy in our house for all things parenting. We've known Kevin for years, up close and personal, and we've seen the positive results of his parenting know-how with his own children. That's why we were thrilled to see this book. We've got two little guys, and this book is sure to give us—and every other parent who reads it—an incredible advantage. Don't miss out on this invaluable message."

— DRS. LES AND LESLIE PARROTT
Founders of RealRelationships.com, authors of *Love Talk*

"Dr. Kevin Leman gives parents the challenge and the tools to raise healthy children in an unhealthy world. Parents will appreciate the humor and practicality of this book."

— GARY D. CHAPMAN, PHD
Best-selling author of *The Five Love Languages of Children*

"Reads like a pep talk from a wise uncle. Dr. Kevin Leman gently encourages parents to remember that there's no substitute for spending time with our kids, and when we do, we're all happier as a family."

— DR. GARY SMALLEY
Author of *Guard Your Child's Heart*

"*It's Your Kid, Not a Gerbil* brings astute psychology and an authentic life of parenting into a resourceful guide for modern-day parents. A must-read for parents looking to defuse the multitude of problems and challenges we face in our society today."

— BOBBY APRIL
Special Teams Coach, Philadelphia Eagles

IT'S YOUR KiD

not a gerbil

Creating a Happier
& Less-Stressed Home

Dr. Kevin Leman

 Tyndale House Publishers, Inc., Carol Stream, Illinois

A Focus on the Family book published by
Tyndale House Publishers, Carol Stream, Illinois 60188

Focus on the Family and the accompanying logo and design are federally registered trademarks of Focus on the Family, Colorado Springs, CO 80995.

TYNDALE and Tyndale's quill logo are registered trademarks of Tyndale House Publishers, Inc.

Some of the content in this book originally appeared in *Home Court Advantage* by Kevin Leman, published by Tyndale House Publishers under ISBN 978-1-58997-464-7.

All Scripture quotations, unless otherwise indicated, are taken from the *Holy Bible, New International Version*®. NIV®. Copyright 1973, 1978, 1984 by Biblica, Inc.™ Used by permission of Zondervan. All rights reserved worldwide. (www.zondervan.com)

Focus on the Family books are available at special quantity discounts when purchased in bulk by corporations, organizations, churches, or groups. For more information, write to: Focus on the Family, 8605 Explorer Drive, Colorado Springs, CO 80920, or call 800-932-9123.

To protect the privacy of those who have shared their stories with the author, some details and names have been changed.

Cover design by Erik M. Peterson
Cover photograph of car copyright © fotoVoyager/iStockphoto. All rights reserved.
Cover photograph of wheel copyright © Willie B. Thomas/iStockphoto. All rights reserved.
Back cover photograph of gerbil copyright © Anna Kucherova/iStockphoto. All rights reserved.
Back cover photograph of girl copyright © ranplett/iStockphoto. All rights reserved.

Library of Congress Cataloging-in-Publication Data
Leman, Kevin.
 It's your kid, not a gerbil : creating a happier and less-stressed home / Kevin Leman.
   p. cm.
 Includes bibliographical references and index.
 ISBN 978-1-58997-615-3 (alk. paper)
 1. Child-rearing—Religious aspects—Christianity. 2. Parenting—Religious aspects—Christianity. 3. Simplicity—Religious aspects—Christianity. 4. Time management—Religious aspects—Christianity. I. Title.
 BV4529.L44 2011
 248.8'45--dc22
                                    2011010407

Printed in the United States of America
1 2 3 4 5 6 7 8 9 / 15 14 13 12 11

*Affectionately dedicated to
my wife, Sande,
who has raised five kids from scratch,
made our house a home,
and has always majored on what's most important.*

CONTENTS

IT'S TIME TO GET OFF THE WHEEL!

Have you ever seen gerbils running on a wheel inside their cage? They sure are intense little creatures, aren't they? And they look so industrious, too—constantly on the move, running with gusto around and around inside that silver circle.

But have you ever considered how tired and bored those little critters must get sometimes, doing the same thing over and over, day after day?

Let's be honest. Isn't that how you feel sometimes as you run from place to place, chauffeuring your children from one endless activity to another?

What if, for one moment, you could just step off the activity wheel . . . and relax? How would you feel then?

And what if that single moment could stretch into an hour, or even a whole day?

There once was a popular ad that featured a woman relaxing in a scented bath and saying, "Calgon, take me away!" If you're feeling as if you could use a little Calgon treatment, isn't it time you gave yourself permission to get off the activity wheel? So your kids can get off that wheel too?

Everybody thinks activities outside the home are good for kids. They help your child develop social networks, allow your child to have new experiences, and even give your child a jump-start over other kids so that he or she will be more successful and even get into the right college . . . or so the reasoning goes.

But have you ever thought about what those activities really mean to your family's schedule and to your together time?

If you want to make a difference in your kid's life, then *you* need to be in your kid's life. No volleyball coach or piano teacher can take your place. And the time spent driving your SUV from point A to point B doesn't count.

I'll tell you a secret: If your kids could pick one person to spend time with, *it would be you.*

You, Mom or Dad. You're the most significant person in your child's life. You provide the loving environment, the security, and the sense of belonging that every child needs to mature into a healthy, well-balanced adult.

But if you're constantly running, you're handing your child's heart and time over to someone who doesn't know—or care—about your child nearly as much as you do.

So many parents today dilute their impact on their own kids be-cause they have fallen for the "busy hands are happy hands" theory. Yet "an August 2003 poll for the Center for a New American Dream, an organization based in Takoma Park, Md., that focuses on quality-of-life issues, revealed that although 60% of Americans felt pressure to work too much, more than 80% wished for more family time and . . . 52% of them would take less money to get it."[1]

If you're among the 80 percent wishing for more family time (and my guess is that the percentage is even higher), you're read-ing the right book. *It's Your Kid, Not a Gerbil* will give you practical solutions and helpful insights to get yourself off the activity wheel so that you can put your time and energies where they really count: establishing strong character and a love for home and family in your kids that will serve them well for a lifetime.

Years from now, when your daughter heads off to college or your son moves into his first apartment, and you say farewell with teary eyes, who do you want them to become? That dream begins by looking forward and carefully cultivating your relationship with your children. *It's Your Kid, Not a Gerbil* will help you lay a firm foundation for a lifetime relationship with your children—kids who are nurtured at home by involved parents, who have downtime, who can say no to peer pressure because they know they belong to your family; kids who are reared for character and not just achievement and who value your faith and standards.

This book is all about that kind of relationship. It's about embracing what matters most and setting priorities to keep your home and family a top priority.

Not only is it doable, but you'll heave a sigh of relief along the way. You'll have more family laughter and less stress, and you'll build memories and relationships your kids will never forget—even when they have homes and families of their own.

You'll never have to think about keeping up with the Joneses again. (Who gave them the right to set the pace for all of us in the first place, I'd like to know?)

Why not live the way you really want to live?

Today's a great day to start.

ONE

IT'S YOUR KID, NOT A GERBIL!

Are you unwittingly upping the ante on your kids—and yourself?

Remember that little gerbil we just talked about? The critter running on the wheel in his cage? I want you to look at him very, very closely. He's running . . . and running . . . and running . . . and . . . running. His heart is going a mile a minute. He's working away, intent on going as far and as fast as he can.

But guess what? That gerbil isn't going anywhere! He can run as hard and as long as he wants, but he'll still be stuck running around on that same wheel day after day, month after month, and perhaps even years, with no end in sight.

That's the state of most kids in America today.

I was recently in a dentist's waiting room and watched a scene play out that's becoming more and more familiar.

A teenage son and his mother entered the waiting room. Both were on their cell phones. The mom was making arrangements, from what I overheard, with a co-worker, to take care of the details of a project while she took her son to the dentist. The son was mute . . . and busy texting. He looked up twice at his mom, as if trying to get her attention, but she was still talking.

So I watched, from my front-row seat next to the son, while he texted his mother: *How long will this take?* When the mother finished talking, she looked at her phone and, rather than answering her son, texted him back: *45 min.*

And they were both right across the room from each other!

Most kids today can text faster than a woodpecker with ADHD. But do they have the relational skills that will bring them satisfaction and fulfillment in life?

David Elkind, author of the groundbreaking books *The Hurried Child* and *All Grown Up and No Place to Go,* says,

> The pressure to grow up fast, to achieve early is very great in middle-class America. There is no room today for the "late bloomer." Children have to achieve success early or they are regarded as losers.[1]

And parents today are driven to make their children "winners." Where did this drive come from?

Take a Little Trip Down Memory Lane . . .

More has changed during the past fifty years than you think, and it has everything to do with how you parent.

Take a look at the 1950s, for instance—the decade of great optimism. Ads from the day that depicted the future showed men and women lounging on the decks of antigravity homes and smiling as they boarded air buses. Back then, people believed that technology would make life a breeze, freeing up more leisure time to spend together.

But is that really what happened? Seems to me that instead of using technology to our advantage, we let technology take advantage of us. Even with all our time-saving inventions, our pace of life has increased. Check out the magazine articles on squeezing the most out of every second, including how to lose weight faster, find the most healthy fast food, and make friends faster. They're all aimed at our "instant" world.

Time, once valued less than money, is now valued *more* than money. While people used to sacrifice time to save money, now they sacrifice money to save time. We pay top dollar for express mail, home grocery delivery service, and one-hour photo development.

And just who do you think is watching? Your kids! What they see Mom or Dad do, they'll also do. (Even if they say during the teenage years that they don't want to be anything like you, guess what? The apple doesn't fall far from the tree!)

Children will always follow your lead. If you are constantly on the go, with a to-do list whose weight would kill an elephant, your children will see that. Interestingly, one study found that time spent on homework more than doubled for six- to eight-year-olds between 1981 and 1997.[2] At Toys"R"Us online, you can even buy PDAs (personal digital assistants) for kids to schedule homework between soccer practice and Cub Scouts. To me, the idea that an elementary-school child would need this is, simply, frightening.

Kids today are stressed at every turn, inundated with material things and experiences in such rapid-fire motion that it would be impossible for them to keep up. As a result, there's increasing concern from teachers, youth leaders, and others who work with children, because more and more kids are feeling burned out by their late teens. Claire, a ten-year-old, told her counselor at school,

> I can never do enough to make my parents happy. They always want more. Mom wants me to make more friends. My dad wants me to be a better student. All I want is to sit by myself in my room and dream sometimes . . . without having to go anywhere.

Claire, by the way, is almost a straight-A student, plays the flute, is on the soccer team at school, is involved in 4-H, takes care of her kindergarten brother for two hours after school until her parents get home, and sometimes even makes dinner for the family.

Superkid—or Superstressed?

The first time you looked into your child's eyes, what did you see?

If you're like most parents, you saw potential . . . and the fulfillment of your dreams. *This kid,* you thought to yourself, *is going to be the best kid ever. Oh, the things she is going to accomplish!*

From that moment on, it's easy to fall into the trap of upping the ante on your child and yourself. The tendency, *especially* for first-time parents, is to try to create a superbaby or supertoddler. So you enroll your child in ballet, play groups, gymnastics, and many other activities—all in the name of good physical activity and "socialization." But it's sort of like reserving a church for your daughter's wedding before she's old enough to date. You're getting way ahead of yourself!

First things first. The most important thing you can do for your child is to allow him or her time to bond with you. Bonding doesn't happen in a day or a month . . . or even a year. It's a slow, steady process based on love, commitment, and time. The more you strengthen that bond between you and your child—by doing fun things together, by playing in the park together, by holding hands with each other—the more you'll create a lifelong bond.

The time of early childhood is precious—kids are so imaginative and such a blast. They're just thrilled to have your attention. Did you know, Mom, that you walk on water in a toddler's eyes? And did you know, Dad, that you are the "biggest, toughest daddy in the whole world," even if you can't bench-press eighty pounds in your wildest dreams? In the eyes of your son or daughter, you are the center of the world.

So don't rush it. Don't up the ante by running from place to place to keep a schedule or by forcing constant socialization with other children through multiple activities. All too soon your child is going to enter preschool or kindergarten and develop other friends outside your family circle. Instead of playing with your child, you'll be watching your child play with someone else. So why hurry the process along? Enjoy the ride—with your child!

And did you know that you're not a rotten parent if you don't enroll your child in preschool? Nobody in my generation went to preschool, and we (at least most of us) seem to be doing just fine. Who says you have to do certain things? Don't fall into the trap of doing what's considered "normal." Why would you want "normal" anyway? If you want a normal child, just look around someday when you're strolling through the mall. You'll find plenty of toddlers throwing tantrums by the carousel horse ride when Momma won't shell out the bucks, preteens sassing their mothers in front of Claire's boutique, and teens giving their parents the eye roll . . . and walking twenty steps behind to make sure they can't be faintly connected to their families. *That's* normal. Is that really what you want?

I didn't think so.

Many people talk as if your kids will be outcasts for life if you don't start them early in a variety of programs to stretch their bodies, minds, and social

Resist the trend to sign up for everything within sight.

skills. Having a friend over to play when your child is three years or younger can be a fun experience, but play groups and play experiences are, in my opinion, vastly overrated. What's far more important is what's happening between you and your child.

If you resist the trend to sign up for everything in sight, you and your child will be better off. In other words, don't sign up your two-year-old for tap dancing because you're worried she doesn't seem very social. Believe me, your child will have plenty of time to socialize with other kids when she's in school. (And you'll have plenty of time to socialize with other parents during all the school activities in the class-room and on field trips.) How your child will relate to those other children will have everything to do with how much she has bonded with you—and how comfortable she feels with herself as a result.

Besides, just wait. By the time your daughter is thirteen, she'll be so social it'll drive you crazy. Every time you pick up the phone, you'll have to suffer through two girls talking—and giggling away—about the secrets of who they think likes whom and who said some-thing *really* dumb in class.

As children get into the school years, they will naturally socialize and develop relationships. Peers will become increasingly important as your child grows. His activity level outside the home will increase each year—and so will yours! After all, who drives him from point A to point B?

So why hurry up the pace any more by upping the ante on your-self and your child? Give yourself and your child quiet downtimes to breathe, to laugh, to take a nap, to just stare out the window, to walk through the fall leaves. There's a big difference between having to run on the activity wheel at times and having to run on it *all the time*, never able to get off. One can be exhilarating; the other is exhausting.

If you're always looking harried and acting stressed from too many activities, if you're constantly talking on your cell phone and running to keep up with an overly busy schedule, and if you're con-stantly late, what are you teaching your child?

That kind of life is frantic and no fun. You have to simply run on the wheel, like that poor gerbil, and you're never able to get off. Is that really the message you want your child to grow up with?

"The Same Thing"—a Good Thing?

I'll make you a deal. Drive into your average elementary-school parking lot for a minute. If you'll give me a five-dollar bill for every

SUV and minivan in the parking lot, I'll give you a twenty-dollar bill for every other kind of car. Who do you think will come out ahead on that one? I bet I will, by far. You know why? Because we humans tend to act like clones. We watch what others are doing, and then we do the same thing. It's part of our human longing for connection, for acceptance. But sometimes "the same thing" isn't a good thing.

We humans tend to act like clones.

Most kids are pushed too hard today. Parents want their kids to be number one at everything they do. If one of their kids comes in second in anything, parents are apt to enroll that child in a special program or give him or her private tutoring and individual lessons to maintain the illusion that their child really is superior in all things.

One of my daughters and her husband are both schoolteachers. Some of the kids who come to their classes are average in intelligence and get average grades—but that's not good enough for Mom and Dad. They create all kinds of waves trying to squeeze something out of their child that just isn't there. But every child is unique—not just another gerbil in a litter. And that child should be treated as unique. Thank goodness we're not all the same! Can you imagine what a boring world that would be?

If you accept your child as she is—and accept that she isn't going to excel at everything—you get both yourself and your child off the endless wheel of expectations.

Just because your neighbor's daughter gets straight As in every subject, does that mean your daughter should, especially if she's an average student?

And just because your best friend's son is involved in five after-school activities a week, does that mean yours should be?

So many of the stresses children face today involve living up to their parents' expectations—and keeping up with running from activity to activity. Your child doesn't need to keep up with the Jones child or the Smith child, or anybody else. But what she does need is a loving parent who can help her discover her uniqueness and her role in the world.

So, parent, don't sell yourself short! You can make a tremendous difference in your kid's life. Offering encouraging and loving words, laughing together, reading together, having meals together, trying new things, and discussing ideas are more important than putting your kid on that gerbil wheel and watching her go around and around and around . . . and get nowhere.

Every kid—even though they're all hedonistic, me-oriented creatures by nature—wants to be part of a family. *Your* family. And home is the place where your child longs to be the most—yes, even when she doesn't act like it.

Think of it this way. When you've been away on a trip, and you're tired, exhausted, and hungry, what's the first thing you think of?

Hey, I think I'll stop by Taco Bell, get a meal deal, and hang out for a while.

Probably not. Most likely, it'll be, *Boy, I can't wait to get home, even if all we have is cereal.*

That same yearning lies within your child. So why not let her be a kid—and not a gerbil? Let her get off the endless wheel . . . and settle in to the comfort of home.

And when you get right down to it, wouldn't *you* rather be home chatting with your daughter over hot cocoa and just-baked cinnamon rolls instead of driving through Starbucks and McDonald's on your way to your second activity of the night? (A hint for those of you who are baking challenged: Swiss Miss and the Pillsbury Doughboy can kick a quiet evening off to a good start!)

You have everything to gain—and nothing to lose—by getting off the activity wheel.

In ten or twenty years, your child won't speak fondly of being driven around town between Girl Scouts, soccer, and gymnastics.

But she will remember with great joy the weekly family pizza night, the Saturday-night Clue games, the Sunday-afternoon movie time, and the warm cookies cooling on the rack when she came home from school.

Good Question!

What kinds of memories do you want your child to have of you, his or her growing-up years, and your home?

How to Get Off the Activity Wheel

- Resist the trend to try to do everything.
- Decide what's best for your family . . . and stick to it.
- Choose activities carefully. Keep life simple.
- Block out time in your schedule just to be home . . . together.

TWO

THE LIGHTS ARE ON, BUT NO ONE'S HOME

*Why home-baked cookies and your presence
matter much more than you think.*

Tricia, a woman in her late thirties, and her two sisters and brother were recently talking about their mom, who had died a couple of years earlier.

"The house wasn't always clean," they admitted, "and the meals certainly weren't gourmet quality most of the time, but Mom was always there for us. She always took the time to listen to us talk about our problems with school, friends, or boys; to ask questions; and to give us back rubs late at night."

What a wonderful thing for your kids to say about you!

This mom certainly wasn't a perfect cook. In fact, the sisters laughed about her lopsided chocolate-chip cookies and her dismal attempts to make Jell-O Jigglers. But they all remembered the wonderful smell of those cookies when they walked in the door after school.

And the brother used to tease his little sister about getting lost in the dust bunnies in the corner of the living room. But this mom put the emphasis where it belonged. She was a nurturing, loving parent, and to this day her kids cherish her memory. Every time they get together, they relive the special moments with their mom, who took their house and made it into a home.

But what if, instead, these siblings had said, "The house was always spic-and-span, and the meals looked like a spread out of *Gourmet* magazine? But you know what? We could never please that woman, could we? It seemed like she was always more concerned about whether we took off our shoes than about how our day went. And if we got a B on a report card or disagreed with something she said, then oh boy, we knew we'd better get away quick!"

What's the difference? It's all in the perspective. Do you think of your abode as a *house* or as a *home*? And does your heart reside there or elsewhere?

One of my favorite speaking engagements is interacting with the women who come to Hearts at Home events. That's because I find women to be amazing creatures. I can never figure out how my wife, Sande, can juggle so magnificently all the things she does. It's enough for me to keep track of one thing at a time. Hearts at Home does an admirable job of giving moms in the trenches encouragement and ideas about how to focus on what's important for the long term—keeping their kids and their homes a priority during their children's growing-up years.

And that's not an easy task, especially for Velcro women. I call women that with the utmost respect, since everything and everyone seem to stick to them, whereas we men seem to float through life just a bit more easily, focusing on one thing at a time. It takes a lot of wading through to-do lists and juggling of schedules and work/career priorities to narrow in on what is truly lasting: a lifelong relationship with your kids.

It also means adjusting your entire perspective toward parenthood and this season of your life.

FedEx Delivery!

Some folks approach the decision to have children with all the emotional investment of joining the buyer's reward program at their favorite grocery store.

One night after driving home their pair of cars from their pair of jobs to their gated-community house, two spouses looked out over the clubhouse swimming pool at a pod of youngsters.

"Maybe we should have some of those . . . you know . . . what do you call them?"

"Children?"

"Yeah, children. Let's have a couple of those."

"Okay—but I'm not going to quit my job."

"Of course not. Nobody does that anymore."

So they order their children, and the package arrives by FedEx nine-month shipping. Their busy schedules continue, seemingly unruffled by this acquisition. They interview caregivers and spend truckloads of money entertaining their brand-new offspring, fresh out of the wrapping.

The dual-track binge continues with the couple trading cars and houses like baseball cards, taking regular vacations to Oahu and other places no one can spell.

Their lives go on, but no one connects.

If you take a look around, that looks like life for a lot of American families, doesn't it? But in your heart of hearts, don't you want your life to be different? Don't you *long* for yours to be different?

Remember the old children's rhyme, "First comes love, then comes marriage, then comes baby in the baby carriage"?

When you first fell in love, your world all of a sudden included another person. It wasn't just *you* that you thought about anymore. That beautiful woman or handsome man now figured prominently in your life. Your center of gravity shifted from just yourself to including someone else.

Then along came the baby carriage, and things *really* started looking different in your family. Your center of gravity shifted again. Life was no longer about just the two of you. Maybe you, Mom, had to shift your workout routine to include breast-feeding and cuddling that infant, or you moved from full-time work to part-time. You, Dad, had to give up babying your car and start babying the baby. Long candlelit evenings at the local Italian restaurant were replaced by midnight drive-through visits to fast-food joints and rush trips to Walgreens for Children's Tylenol.

All that to say, life goes on when kids arrive, but it sure doesn't go on the same way! For many parents, this can be a tough transition. In today's instant and driven world, kids are tremendously time consuming.

But as a father of five, I'll let you in on a secret. Parenting is worth every minute of time that you invest. Sande and I wouldn't trade even one of our five kids in for another model. Each is wonderfully unique and now contributing in amazing ways to the world. We're convinced it has everything to do with our determined focus on home relationships first, above anything else.

A Sense of Belonging

Zenith used to have a great ad for its TVs that proclaimed, "The quality goes in before the name goes on." How right they were!

I've always told my kids that if they ever wonder what to do in a certain situation, they should remember, *You're a Leman.*

What do I mean by that? Saying "You're a Leman" means I'm telling my kids, "You belong to this family, and you know our values. So stand up for yourself. Remember who you are. Don't let anybody jack you around."

Time and again our kids have thanked Sande and me for that reminder. Knowing who they are has enabled them to say, in tough situations with their peers, "No, I don't want to try smoking. I'm a Leman. Lemans don't smoke," and "No, I don't drink. I'm a Leman, and Lemans don't drink." Having the family label, knowing that they belong to this family and represent this family and our values has taken my kids out of harm's way more times than I'll probably ever know. It would take a pretty gutsy peer to come back and argue over that response, knowing that dear ol' Dad and Momma Bear stand behind it.

> **I've always told my kids that if they ever wonder what to do in a certain situation, they should remember, You're a Leman.**

Keeping your child off the activity wheel and focused on your home and values builds in your child a strong character, a foundation of belonging, and a very high chance that he or she will grow into a healthy, caring, and mature adult. Now that's a distinct advantage that lasts for a lifetime.

A Lifetime Platinum Member

If I'm on an airplane, two things are probably true. First, I'm sitting in the front row. That's because I get a bit claustrophobic, and after flying more than five million miles, it's the least my airline can do to allow me a little extra space.

Second, the words *American Airlines* are painted on the tin can I'm flying in. I've been a frequent flyer with American since 1988. Early on, I flew other airlines as well, but now, as long as American can accommodate me, I'm pretty loyal to this one airline.

Why? Because I feel at home with American Airlines. Infrequent flyers can sign up for the frequent-flyer program, but they get credited with their actual miles. Me? I get *double miles* wherever I go, which add up pretty fast. Plus, on occasion I get free upgrades—even free tickets!

And when my schedule changes, American goes out of its way to please me. You might get to the airport three hours before I do to get your name on the standby list in hopes of catching an earlier flight. I might show up just thirty minutes before the plane pushes back, but I'm the one who gets the seat. Why? With more than five million miles logged on my account, I'm what they call a "Lifetime Platinum" member, which is airline-speak for "Please this sucker at all costs, because he's spent enough on plane tickets over the years to buy the plane he's flying on."

In short, when I'm flying American, I have a distinct advantage. If I step onto a United flight, or a Delta flight, or a Southwest flight, I'm Joe Schmo. I'll get the same packet of peanuts as everyone else. Some other lug will get the good seat up front. And I might even be stuck in a middle seat, which at my age and size feels like a rhinoceros being crammed into Tweety Bird's cage.

When Dorothy clicked her heels in *The Wizard of Oz* and said over and over, "There's no place like home. There's no place like home," she was right.

It's a nice feeling to live life on American Airlines as a Lifetime Platinum member.

Wouldn't you like to give your kids the same sense of security and joy and even happiness? Wouldn't you like them to feel that being born into your family has given them something special? Wouldn't you like them to be as loyal to you as I am to American?

When Dorothy clicked her heels in *The Wizard of Oz* and said over and over, "There's no place like home. There's no place like home," she was right. There is no place like home.

If your kids see home as a place of security, joy, and good memories, they'll want to come back, even when they're grown up. They'll remember the best part of their lives as happening within the four walls of that blessed place spelled H-O-M-E.

But it all starts with you. Is home where your heart is? Where your priorities are? Or do you let opportunities and to-do lists take you away from the one place that matters more than anyplace else to your child?

Who's Home?

Did you know that, on average, fathers communicate with their teenage children just thirty-five minutes per week?[1] Thirty-five minutes! I spend more time than that picking lint from my belly button. And it isn't just fathers who are absent from their children's lives. Another study, published in *Time* magazine, found that "72% of women with children under 18 are in the work force—a figure that is up sharply from 47% in 1975."[2] The reasons for parents' absence may be complex, but the bottom line is that they *are* absent.

Some families have legitimate reasons for not having a parent at home with the children. Another article in the same issue of *Time* stated, "Since the mid-'70s, the amount of the average family budget earmarked for the mortgage has increased a whopping 69% (adjusted for inflation). At the same time, the average father's income increased less than 1%."[3]

Often, Mom picks up the slack by jumping into the marketplace. And many single parents are the sole breadwinners, so not working isn't an option.

But many of the families I see as I travel throughout the country have their children in childcare for other reasons. It's not because they have no options, such as enlisting family or co-op childcare or adopting a less expensive standard of living. It's because they have other priorities: climbing the corporate ladder or keeping up with the Joneses. Many parents use childcare to stay in the rat race instead of considering the options of Dad or Mom staying home even part-time.

The most important thing you can give your child is your presence.

The American dream—of having a house, two kids, two cars, and two upwardly mobile jobs—is an alluring one. But at what cost? The most important thing you can give your child is your presence. Without you, that better house in a nicer neighborhood isn't a home. It's merely a house.

Think of it this way. Anytime you're handing your child over to anyone else for care—especially in the first six years of life—you're missing thousands of opportunities to imprint positive values on your child's character.

Can day care give your child a safe place to play? Yes. Can it provide a positive place for social interaction? Yes. Can it provide a basis for a good education? Yes. Can it reinforce your values and your faith? If you choose your day-care provider carefully, maybe. But day-care workers can't do what's most important: nurturing a lifetime relationship between you and your child.

Some of you are currently working outside the home. I want you to know that I'm not saying any of this to make you feel guilty. Some of you are in situations where you have to work outside the home right now. There isn't another option.

All I'm asking is that you examine the time you spend away from home. *Why* do you do so? Is it really because you have to, or is it because you've embraced more opportunities than you can manage and have locked yourself into a tyrannical schedule?

All of us have the same twenty-four hours in a day. Why not commit to making the most of what you have in a way that will influence your children for a lifetime?

Making time to be with your kids takes sacrifice. Sande and I lived on a shoestring for years so that she could be at home with our five children. When my oldest daughter, Krissy, and her husband, Dennis, had their first child, they made the difficult decision to pare back their living standards so Krissy could stay at home. Roger and Connie made a different decision. He left his downtown Milwaukee office and cut his office hours to part-time so he could stay at home with their two young children, since Connie's full-time job involved a lot of travel. And she cut back her traveling so that she's gone only five days a month.

No one can take your place.

Every sacrifice you make now will pay dividends both now and down the road. That's because a child's positive self-image, view of the world, concept of faith, and sense of security are all formed by spending time with parents in a loving environment. And no one can take your place.

What Every Kid Wants

My love for fishing is almost innate. We have photos of me as a child wearing my father's knee boots as hip waders. My mother, who recognized my passion early on, would walk me the quarter mile to Ellicott Creek almost every summer day until I grew old enough to go there myself with my little fishing pole and worms wriggling in my pocket.

Though Ellicott Creek gave me untold hours of pleasure, the one thing it didn't have was trout. Trout season, which opened in western New York on April 1, always held a mystique for me as a boy; I'd never caught a trout in my life. After every opening day, the local newspaper ran a photograph showing trout fishermen lined up elbow to elbow, with so many lines in the water, they could have woven a net. I wanted to join them.

One year, the day after that picture appeared in the paper, I walked into a sporting-goods store and for sixty cents bought a little plastic lure in the shape of a hellgrammite, a multilegged bug. I still recall asking my father if he would take me to that trout stream in the photo. It was probably ten to fifteen miles away as the crow flies, certainly more than a nine-year-old boy could walk.

My father had an eighth-grade education, worked hard in the dry-cleaning business, and didn't have much leisure time. As a result, he almost never went fishing. I wanted so badly for him to go that day, but he couldn't—or wouldn't.

So I made the familiar trip down to Ellicott Creek myself and began fishing for trout, knowing full well that there weren't any there. I stood the entire day in a flooded creek that was so murky, the trout wouldn't have been able to find the hook even if they'd miraculously showed up hungry.

My father, perhaps unwittingly, made a painful memory in my life. And that memory has stuck strongly with me to this day, more than half a century later.

Your kid may come up to you with a request that seems silly, far-fetched, or just bothersome. Without even thinking about it, you may say, "Not now, honey," or "Maybe next week," or "Why don't you just go play on your Xbox?" You may never think about that request again.

But that doesn't mean your child will forget it.

I don't bear any ill will toward my father. Being a father myself now, I'm sure he forgot about my request less than three hours after I made it. He didn't realize he was making a memory.

But I hope *you* do. Is that the kind of memory you want your kids to have of you?

Your garage may need cleaning. Your car may need waxing. But are those chores really more important in the long-term than helping Junior patch together a cardboard rocket he's planning on flying to the moon? Behind those childish ways is a heart that wants little else than to spend time with *you*. That makes you, Dad, and you, Mom, special individuals indeed.

Believe it or not, this is true even of adolescents. When U.S. teens were asked where they'd most like to spend more time, hanging out with their families was the top choice over visiting with friends, playing sports, working out, watching TV, or surfing the Web.

Your kids aren't all that interested in your promotion to vice president of marketing. They aren't interested in how your presentation went in Chicago. They aren't interested in your bridge score or how much Mary Kay product you sold last quarter.

They *are* interested in whether you're at their ball game when they hit their first line-drive single, or whether you're in the elementary-school auditorium to hear them scratch out that violin solo you've endured at home for the past seven weeks. They care that you tell them their favorite story—the unabridged version—at bedtime over and over and over again, and that you see them manage to stay up on two wheels for more than twenty feet as they learn to ride the bicycle, and that you kiss their skinned elbows when they fall down.

Time together makes all the difference.

Time together makes all the difference.

I heard of a boy in a progressive school who was taking part in individualized education. One day he said, "Hey, can we have one of those days when we . . . um . . . when we used to . . . you know . . ."—he stumbled as he searched for the right word—"talk? That's it! Could we just *talk* again?"

Statistics show that most kids want exactly that—to "just talk again" with their parents. According to George Barna's survey results in his book *Real Teens,*

The most common substantive changes suggested [by teens regarding their relationship with their fathers] were the need to spend more time together (mentioned by 19 percent), . . . [and] wanting better communication (13 percent).[4]

Beneath their PlayStation-playing, MP3-music-collecting, DVD-watching behavior, that's really what your kids want.

A Child's Number One

One spring Bill Cosby and I were asked to participate in a presentation on preventing violence for an audience of ten thousand people in Oklahoma City. I was Cosby's opening act, though I conned myself into thinking that they'd really come to see me.

Before the program, after we'd hammed it up for pictures and completed the handshaking, I spent a half hour backstage alone with Cosby. He's a Temple Owls fan, and I'm an Arizona Wildcats fan, so we hit it off by talking about basketball. After a while, our talk turned to the topic of the evening—the influence of families on today's youth.

Parents—not drugs, not movies, not peer groups—are a child's number-one influence.

Cosby, whose son had been violently murdered, wanted to know what I thought about what was happening to families in our society today. The answer we discussed backstage emerged time and again that evening in our interaction with the audience. Parents—not drugs, not movies, not peer groups—are a child's number-one influence.

It came as no surprise to me. But in a culture in which we complain about all the influences on a child's life, it's important to remember that parents *are* what make the difference. Your words, your silence, your presence, your absence, your example—both good and bad—all matter more in the life of your child than you may ever realize.

Why am I so sure? Well, let me tell you a bit of my own life story.

I'll Be Home for Christmas

At nineteen years of age, I packed my bags and left home. At the time I lived with my parents in Arizona, but I *hated* Arizona. A buddy back in New York had told me I could live with him for a while, so I packed up and headed cross-country to his house, foot-loose and fancy-free. Unfortunately, my friend was good at drinking beer and lousy at following through on his word.

I arrived after dark in my 1950 Ford. My friend's parents were still awake, judging by the light inside. I didn't feel comfortable introducing myself and explaining that I would be staying with them. I decided to wait; my buddy was supposed to meet me there at 11:30 p.m., after he finished work. Finally the lights winked off as his parents turned in for the night.

Eleven thirty came and went. The temperature dropped, which would have been bearable, except that my beloved Ford had no heater. The minutes sleepwalked slowly into morning as I sat shivering, freezing my Rumpelstiltskin off.

That night I had plenty of time to think. When I closed my eyes and pulled my jacket around me, I imagined slipping under that comforter on my bed in my parents' home, twenty-five hundred miles away. I would have paid a lot of money to be in that place I'd taken for granted.

Eventually I came to realize that my parents' undying love and support had made all the difference in my life. Finally it drew me back home.

Maybe that's why the song "I'll Be Home for Christmas" always makes me cry. It's a melancholy piece of music that reminds me of the simple gift of home and good times with my family growing up. It wasn't a perfect home—my dad was an alcoholic. But it *was* a good home.

Your home might not be perfect either. But you can do everything in your power to make home the place your child will dream about when he or she is away.

The place where your child most wants to be.

Home Is Where the Heart Is

When I'm standing in front of a group of people, and I say, "Everybody point to yourself," 999 out of a 1,000 will point right to their hearts. Your biggest job as a parent is to capture your child's heart. You need to know your child's heart, help train your child's heart, protect your child's heart, and listen to your child's heart.

To be a good parent, you don't have to be superhuman. You don't have to be Mom of the Year or Dad of the Year. You don't have

Your biggest job as a parent is to capture your child's heart.

to be a gourmet cook or the PTA president. As I often tell moms and dads, you can be a bird, you can be a plane, but whatever you do, don't try to be Superparent! If you do, you'll fail. No one can fly on the Superparent track for long without taking a nosedive or crash-landing.

So instead of worrying about what you *can't* do, be confident of what you *can* do. Why not spend your hours where they can make the most difference in the long haul?

Imagine if you asked your kids this question: "What do you remember most about when you were younger?" How would they answer?

Of course, your ten-year-old, who considers himself grown up, may remember back to when he was five, and you let him stay up late—9:00 p.m.—and play with his special new toys when he had the measles. And your fourteen-year-old? Maybe she'll remember all the nights you've tucked her into bed and talked about something special that happened for each of you that day.

Twenty years from now, your kids won't remember the four-thousand-dollar trip you took to Disney World. Not really. But they'll remember the simple things. The times that involve you, Mom or Dad.

Indeed, your presence in your child's life matters . . . much more than you could ever imagine. And the benefits of your time, well spent, will last for a lifetime.

Good Question!

How might you cut back in one area to spend more time together as a family?

Priority Check

- Realize you can't have it all.
- Evaluate how much time you're spending—or not spending—with your family.
- Choose your priorities wisely and commit to sticking to them.
- Ask yourself each evening, Am I truly living out those priorities? In what areas am I not?
- Take time to capture your child's heart.

THREE

BUSY IS GOOD, RIGHT? (AND OTHER MYTHS)

Why stacking up activities to ramp up your kid's success in life won't get you where you want to go.

Visit any Baskin-Robbins, and you'll be dazzled by thirty-one flavors of ice cream to choose from—everything from the usual mint chocolate chip and strawberry flavors to pistachio, moose tracks, and bubble gum. The store is a little bit of heaven for ice-cream lovers of all ages. No wonder it's jam-packed every summer day.

The Baskin-Robbins of Life, though, doesn't offer just thirty-one unique activities—it offers thirty-one thousand, and we parents drool over the options like kids at an ice-cream counter. After all, keeping your kids busy is good, right? And with so many wonderful activities to choose from, how could you go wrong? Aren't all these activities fine-tuning your child's development and pushing him or her ahead of the rest of the pack?

Well, what do you think?

Quiz time! Which of the following nine statements are true, and which are false?

1. It's not the quantity of time with my kids that matters; it's the quality.
2. I'm a good parent if I make many sacrifices for my child.

3. Children should be free to express themselves any way they want.
4. My child deserves the things I didn't have growing up, the things most kids today have.
5. A full plate of activities is good for kids; let them absorb all they can.
6. A gifted child is a successful child.
7. Starting kids early in school will give them an extra edge.
8. In today's competitive world, it's important that a child finish first.
9. If children set their minds to it, they can do anything.

Did you find yourself answering *true* to any of these statements? If so, you've fallen for one or more of today's popular parenting myths. But don't feel bad—we all do. Even if you caught on and answered *false* to every statement, you may have secretly thought, *Now, what's wrong with* that, *Dr. Leman?*

In this chapter, we'll examine five of these myths and learn why it's so easy to fall for them. (We'll look at the final four myths in the next chapter.) It isn't until you realize why you're falling for them that you can get yourself and your kids off that crazy activity wheel.

Myth No. 1: "It's Not the Quantity of Time with My Kids That Matters; It's the Quality"

"Great news!" a husband calls to his wife as he heads out the front door with his golf clubs slung over his shoulder. "The Smiths have agreed to videotape Clovis's piano recital while I'm on the course with the new client. I honestly didn't know how I'd pull it off, but somehow I managed. I'll be back this evening to tuck Clovis in!"

Trust me—when nervous little Clovis looks into the audience before his recital and sees the reflecting glass of the video-camera lens instead of his father's caring eyes, it's not going to be much consolation. Especially if Dad already told Clovis he'd be there.

"But it was just *like* being there!" Dad might argue. "I made sure Mr. Smith caught everything on tape!"

What Dad doesn't realize is that although *he* may have felt he was there, his absence felt like a huge black hole for Clovis. It was a screaming statement of noninterest and poor priorities.

Oh yeah. Dad shouldn't be surprised if when he tries to tuck little Clovis in tonight, the boy pretends to already be asleep.

You can't cheat a child in your priorities and then somehow make it up with a bit of "quality time," which is almost always defined by the parent's convenience and availability, not the kid's preference. Even children who can't divide ten by two can be razor sharp when it comes to the mathematics of priority. Even if you *are* able to fool them for a little while with trinkets brought back from business trips, eventually they'll figure out what those "souvenirs" cost them: time with you.

> **Even children who can't divide ten by two can be razor sharp when it comes to the mathematics of priority.**

I've talked to thousands of children, and one thing has come through crystal clear in our conversations: Rushed love doesn't feel like love to a child. If your child feels as if she's "on the clock," or if she thinks she's always interrupting you, *love* won't be the first word that comes to her mind when she thinks back on her childhood.

In a society frenzied with activity, time together at home is more important than ever. If you're focused on helping your kids "get ahead," you're bypassing the most important factor of their development—leisurely love and gracious attention at home, far from a hurried and harried world.

A toddler doesn't think abstractly. He sees that you're around or you aren't. Whether you're away at work, on the golf course, or volunteering at your church doesn't really make much difference. All that registers in your child's little brain is that you're there or not. And yes, he is asking the question, "If Dad (or Mom) really loves me like he says he does, why doesn't he want to spend more time with me?"

Generally speaking, the more your child spends time with you, the more stability and less uncertainty there will be in his life. This doesn't mean you should make your child the center of the universe, but your regular physical and emotional presence, even in small ways, makes a big difference.

Okay, so by now some of you may be feeling guilty. Well, you can feel guilty . . . or you can see what I'm saying as an opportunity. Imagine the impact you can have by taking your young son or daughter out to lunch every other week or so. Or instead of sitting in your favorite chair with your face behind the newspaper, why not read it with your child at the table and discuss it? My daughter Holly and I read *USA Today* together every morning for years; I reached for the sports section, and she got the entertainment section. She still talks about those times with great fondness.

When I was growing up, my father scratched my back while we watched TV together. Halfway through a thirty-minute program, we'd switch and I'd scratch his back. I value the memory of those times more than I do any car I've owned or any house I've bought. Even kids who didn't get enough of their parents, or who came from troubled homes, cherish the few good moments they did have.

Quality time does not make up for quantity time. If you believe that myth, then you're doing so to rationalize your own selfish behavior. *Ouch*, I know, but I had to say it because it's true. So many parents are committed to chasing their own rainbows—maintaining a perfect home, following every sports event aired on ESPN (while watching ESPN2 and ESPN Classic during the commercials), even garnering peer approval for their involvement in church, school, or community activities. And their kids? Well, they'll just have to fit into the parents' schedule, won't they?

But for a child, the *quantity* of time you spend together is part of what makes it a *quality* experience. If after dinner tonight, you were to set before your three-year-old child a very small single scoop of Godiva Belgian dark-chocolate ice cream in one bowl and a large mixing bowl heaped high with your local supermarket's freezer-burned brand in the other, which would he or she choose? The heaping bowlful, of course. For kids,

> **For kids, quantity matters. That's why kids can smell their way blindfolded to any all-you-can-eat pizza place in town.**

quantity matters. That's why kids can smell their way blindfolded to any all-you-can-eat pizza place in town.

Yes, quantity time should be quality time, too—more than simply logging minutes in the parent-child flight book. But *more* is part of the equation that makes time with you *better*. Traveling sports teams and after-school clubs may be stimulating and educational, but signing your child up for even three of these activities simultaneously cuts quantity *and* quality. The *advantage* comes from being at *home*, developing the relationship between parent and child, as well as sibling and sibling, and you can't do that on the road.

Myth No. 2: "I'm a Good Parent if I Make Many Sacrifices for My Child"

I was on the phone with one seven-year-old's parents. They'd given their son the world. Unfortunately, he was relishing the role of tyrannical little Julius Caesar.

At first glance, you might be surprised. This was a tight-knit family with a strong faith, and the parents wanted nothing more than for their son to succeed. In fact, his success was the basket into which they'd piled all their eggs. They'd given him every opportunity on the face of the earth and even prepared him for one or two beyond—space camp, for example, when he was only four years old.

They couldn't understand why their son, rather than embracing the ambitions of a future astronaut, was hatching into a little alien. He was well behaved in school but didn't finish any work. And at home he was beginning to mouth off at Mom and Dad.

As I talked with them, it quickly became evident that the problem wasn't that they'd been uninvolved in his life. They'd *overdone* it.

Fully half of the parents who've walked through my counseling door have overparented—either because of perfectionist expectations or simply because they'd been revolving around their child as if she were the center of the family's universe.

Overparent? you may think. *How can you overdo it on love?*

When you overparent, you weaken your child's self-image, suffocating her so that your child comes to believe, *I guess I don't have what it takes to get by without Dad's and Mom's help. They obviously don't believe I can finish anything by myself, so it's probably better not to complete things. Then they can't criticize my unfinished project or me.* The child may not say or even consciously think that, but that's what's going on.

Some parents think they're sacrificing when they overparent. What they're really doing, though, is hovering.

Imagine a hovering boss with impossibly high standards. After a few months of working for him, you'd sink into your chair at seeing that shadow across your shoulder. You'd dread new projects and start dreaming of jobs in more relaxing fields, such as point person on the bomb squad or air-traffic controller at the world's busiest airport. Is that really how you want your kids to look at you, jumping whenever you enter the room, dreading that "tsk, tsk" as you look over their shoulders?

A hover boss's attitude says, "You'll fail without my constant supervision." The "sacrificing" perfectionist parent sends the same message.

Hovering can happen so innocently, too. Little Buford, having stubbed his toe, may be hanging on to Mommy's leg to get her attention. So what does Mommy do? She picks Buford up, comforts him, and perhaps overdoes it a bit in the process. Next time Buford gets hurt, he'll expect the same emergency-room care—complete with the Popsicle to make him feel better! And it only ramps up from there.

Overdo it enough, and you'll reinforce habits you don't want to instill in your child. After all, children are born thinking about *me, me, me*. It's your job as a parent to help them begin to consider others before themselves. You don't want to create habits that last into your child's graduate-school education or marriage. (Believe me, your daughter-in-law or son-in-law will thank you someday if you hang in there and fight this myth.)

When does your "help" hurt your kids? When you do things they can do for themselves. When my kids were young, I used to pour milk from the big gallon jug onto their cereal for them. As they grew up, when they could do it themselves—with minimal splashing!—I encouraged them to do just that. Did that mean I didn't care? Far from it! I was allowing them to build their own self-worth by doing something they could do.

But let's say your fifteen-year-old decides she's not going to follow through on a commitment. She wants you to make a phone call for her, announcing that she's backing out. In that instance I'd say, "*You* call Mrs. Johnson and tell her that you're unable to babysit. You're the one who told her you would. You call and tell her you can't."

Making that call on her behalf might feel like love, but it would only stunt her growth. The "sacrifice" wouldn't do either of you any good.

So don't do your kid's dirty work. If your child consistently leaves projects undone or approaches tasks with all the enthusiasm of an anesthetized sloth, he or she may be under the shadow of a hovering parent.

As for that father and mother of the junior Julius Caesar, I told them to exercise the courage to be imperfect parents—doctor's orders. They were simply trying too hard to do everything. Their boy was bright but would waste his academic years if they didn't back off and let him repeat second grade.

Often the best sacrifice you can make for your child is relinquishing your own subtle expectations.

Myth No. 3: "Children Should Be Free to Express Themselves Any Way They Want"

Sande and I were in a restaurant with a woman we hadn't seen in years. She'd brought her two little boys with her, and they were cuter than cute, the kind you'd find on a breakfast-cereal commercial or a Saturday-morning kids' show. But like stereotypical child stars, they were unmanageable.

One of them, a four-year-old, was clearly trained in torture techniques. He began digging his fingernails into my leg under the table. Perhaps it was my contorted face that caused Mommy to try to divert his attention. In response, he started hitting her.

"Oh, that's boys for you!" the woman said as she tickled her son to make light of his behavior.

Lady, I thought, *boys* are *different from girls. But boys and girls alike need discipline!*

All kids need lines drawn in the sand to know what is simply not acceptable. They need to know they can't hit, hold their sisters hostage, or stage a minivan mutiny.

I'm all for nurturing kids' personalities and gifts. But anyone who believes that children are born with angel wings should toss a candy bar into the Duck, Duck, Goose circle and watch as the little devils come out. Boundaries have to be drawn. You don't really want to encourage *all* that your children are, do you? Stop and think about *that* for a minute.

My good friend Dr. James Dobson often talks about the research study in which a school tore down its playground fences so kids wouldn't feel confined. Instead of playing right up to where the fences had been, however, children clustered in the center of the open school yard.[1] You see, kids draw strength, stability, and self-esteem from boundaries, because boundaries help define what is safe and what isn't.

Anyone who believes that children are born with angel wings should toss a candy bar into the Duck, Duck, Goose circle and watch as the little devils come out.

Many parents today want their kids to be whoever they are, without any constraints. But whenever kids take the reins, families end up in a mess—and then they come to my counseling office to sort it all out. Now's the time to take the reins—or take back the reins if you've been allowing your kids to hold them.

Don't relinquish the responsibility for parenting your kids to the "experts," the media, or your child's teachers—let alone your child.

Stand up and be a parent!

Myth No. 4: "My Child Deserves the Things I Didn't Have Growing Up, the Things Most Kids Today Have"

When our daughter Lauren decided to try out for the school softball team, we encouraged her to follow that dream.

But we didn't jump in and drop five hundred dollars to buy the latest equipment or another five hundred for lessons with a softball pro to get her through the tryouts. She used her older sister's mitt, and since there was already enough aluminum leaning against the dugout walls to build an entire house, we figured she didn't need to own a bat. There were plenty to borrow.

Lauren made the team. Soon after practices started, she opened a dinner conversation by saying, "Dad, I need to get spikes."

Notice the wording: not "*May* I have spikes," but "I *need* to get spikes."

"Oh really?" I said. "You know, honey, I played ball for a long time—even made the all-star team—and I didn't have spikes."

"But everybody else has them!" Lauren said.

"Well, we'll see," I said.

I purposely didn't give her a definite answer. Instead, I went to her practices and saw that while some of the kids did have cleats, quite a few didn't. As the first game grew closer, though, all the girls except Lauren got baseball shoes. Some looked so geared-up you'd have thought they were playing for the Arizona Diamondbacks.

I still didn't buy Lauren cleats. Before you tell me what a terrible father I am, let me assure you: I'm well aware of what not having something "everyone else" does can do to a seventy-pound kid; it can create a hundred pounds of peer pressure. So why didn't I buy the shoes?

Because Lauren's argument was "Dad! *Everyone else* has them."

I agreed aloud with Lauren that everybody else had baseball shoes. "But I don't want you to be like everybody else," I explained.

You see, if Lauren is like "everybody else," then there's a very high probability she'll experiment with drugs and lose her virginity before she gets her high-school diploma. Being like everybody else is about the *worst* argument she could feed me!

Money wasn't the main issue with Lauren's plea for the cleats. *Being like everybody else was.*

By now you're probably thinking, *Oh, c'mon, Dr. Leman. Cleats? That's a small thing. If you can afford it, why not?*

Here's why: I didn't want my child to expect that when she joins the hobby-of-the-month club, I'll fully outfit her with the latest high-tech gear. Young kids change their interests more frequently than their underwear. If you buy all the equipment every time, you'll soon be opening a used sporting-goods store in your garage. That goes for American Girl dolls, Pokémon cards, and other toys, too. Buy the latest one, and you'll soon discover that it's collecting a heap of dust in the corner of your kid's room—right next to all the other things you bought her six months ago. If you meet her every desire, you're training her to believe that whenever she wants something, all she has to do is turn to Dad or Mom, and you'll get it for her.

And just how well do you think that's going to work someday when your kid is out of the nest, is earning entry-level pay at her first job, and has begun racking up bills on her first credit card because she still has to have the latest and the greatest?

> **The way you respond to the latest and the greatest "stuff" now will set a pattern for your child's lifetime.**

The way you respond to the latest and the greatest "stuff" now will set a pattern for your child's lifetime. Are you always going to go along with the crowd and do what "everybody else" does, even if it doesn't make sense?

As for Lauren and softball, I wanted to wait a year to see if she was going to stick with it. If she did, I might even have shelled out a few bucks and bought her a new mitt, as well as some softball shoes. Maybe. (My kids call me cheap, but I prefer to think of myself as economical.)

You might think I'm an ogre for allowing my daughter to play softball in tennis shoes. *What a deprived kid,* you're thinking as you're inwardly *tsk-tsking.*

But let me tell you something. During that year, Lauren's face lit up when she came home. She'd run to me and say, "Dad, you gotta pitch to me and throw me some fly balls."

So I'd get out my ridiculously old mitt, which she'd laugh at, and we'd have a good time creating memories that would last a hundred times longer than a size 6 pair of spikes.

Shelling out sixty dollars for a pair of baseball shoes doesn't require much commitment or sacrifice. But committing to be home before Lauren arrives, and being free to practice with her—that requires a bit more.

You want to know something else? Lauren forgot about the shoes. Once her teammates got used to seeing her in tennis shoes, it was no big deal. No one mentioned it; no one bugged her. They just enjoyed playing together as a team.

It comes down to this solid truth: What you give your kids doesn't mean that much. What does matter? Your commitment. Your presence. Your input.

Lauren will soon graduate from high school. Not having softball shoes doesn't matter a lick to her anymore. In fact, she laughs about it when she remembers that time. So her dad wouldn't pay sixty dollars for her shoes. There's something far more important ingrained in her mind: She knows her dad would lay down his life for her. If she needed a kidney transplant, I'd be first in line, even if it was my last kidney. Blood transfusion? Drain me dry if that's what it takes. Because I'm committed to my not-so-little girl . . . for a lifetime. And our relationship, *not the stuff I can give her*, is what counts.

Today Lauren doesn't need "stuff" to be like everyone else. She's a strong-minded, compassionate, multitasking young woman who is her own person. She doesn't need "stuff" to make her who she is. And now she thinks through her own decisions very carefully— *Do I really need that? Nah.* And then she doesn't give it another thought.

So don't fall for the line that if you love your kids, you'll give them everything they want—as long as you can afford it. Don't fear that if you don't give your kids what others have, they'll resent you (if they do, you have more than "stuff" to work on in your family!), or they'll fall behind their peers.

I'm far more interested in cultivating realistic expectations and thankful hearts.

Does that mean you don't get your kids anything? No, I didn't say that. What's important is that you think through your decisions carefully, and that you give in moderation.

For example, when our daughter Hannah turned sixteen, we still had a steam-powered computer that she used to do her homework and e-mail friends. It was slower than molasses running uphill, and it had less memory than a two-day-old baby.

"Dad," my son, Kevin II, said, "in two years Hannah's heading off to college, and she'll need a computer. The one we have now is so old, it won't run any of the new programs she's going to need. Why don't you consider getting her a notebook computer? An Apple iBook would be a great choice."

Sande and I knew more about quantum physics and ancient Aramaic than we did about computers—which is to say, nothing at all. At that time, to me, a hard drive was a difficult commute home, and I wouldn't think of burning a DVD without a permit from the fire department. But Kevin II knew his stuff. (Thank goodness someone in this family did!)

Hannah was thrilled. She got a computer without even asking for it! Not once did she ever say with an attitude, "I want a computer!" I guess brothers are good for something after all.

"Did you see the note?" Sande asked me the morning after we'd given Hannah her computer. I walked into the kitchen, and there was a note on a paper plate:

I just want to thank you again. I love you guys so much; thank you for my computer. —Your Hannah

Your Hannah.

Now that's a phrase to shoot for when you're building a lifetime relationship with your child. It's the kind of thing worth writing—or e-mailing—home about.

When I needed a new computer (uh, does it mean something when you turn your old computer on, and it starts to smell like burned rubber?), I called Kevin II, the family expert. And once more, he rose to the occasion.

Now if only I could figure out how to work the computer's flimsy slide-out cup holder . . .

Myth No. 5: "A Full Plate of Activities Is Good for Kids; Let Them Absorb All They Can"

A *Newsweek* article described the overflowing plate of one teenager:

> As captain of the junior-varsity volleyball team, first-chair flute in the school orchestra, a top player on the tennis team and an honors student with three hours of homework a night, Andrea Galambos, who was also taking singing and art classes after school, put in 18-hour days. "I never had more than five minutes to sit down and breathe," says Andrea, 16, a junior at Staples High School in Westport [Connecticut]. Some mornings she didn't want to get out of bed because of all the stuff she had to do.[2]

I couldn't make up a worse recipe for a balanced and fulfilling home life if I tried.

Many kids' activity schedules rival an Olympic athlete's training routine. Some parents take pride in this overcommitment because they're running so hard on the wheel themselves that they wear their busyness like an Olympic medal. Unfortunately, they end up pulling their kids along on that same crazily spinning wheel of activities.

Are You on the Activity Wheel?

Questions and guilt reducers, especially for moms (the Wonder Women of the family schedule):

1. Am I getting myself and my child involved in too many activities? Am I so focused on scheduling playtime, music time, recreational time, art time, or any other activity time for my child, that I scarcely have time to think or rest?
   (Remember, Mom, if you're tired, you're not going to be at your best—and you'll probably take it out on your children, because that's who you're with most of the time.)

2. Am I trying to be the perfect mom, or am I focusing on being an excellent mom? Am I asking too much of myself?
   (Parenting is a twenty-four-hours-a-day, eighteen-plus-years job. Nobody hits grand slams every time he gets up to bat. Give yourself a break; you're going to have good days and bad days. If you harp on yourself because you had one bad day, or one frustrated outburst, you'll drive yourself crazy with guilt.)

3. Am I a slave to my to-do list? Do I act like it's a crime if I have to let laundry go or allow a room to get messy?
   (It's okay to occasionally leave a few dirty dishes in the sink while you tend to more important matters. The Dirty Dish Police won't show up at your door. I promise. [That's because when Sande's away, they're always at mine.])

4. Am I obsessed with what others think of me? Do I put too much time and effort into what kinds of clothes my kids are wearing and the things they have so that everyone will think I'm the perfect mom?
   (The more important question is really, Why do you think you have to be the perfect mom? No one's perfect. Not the principal of your child's school. Not the CEO who lives next door and lets his grass grow waist high. Not the dishwasher repair technician. So why should you expect yourself to be perfect? The old proverb "To err is human" is right. So cut yourself some slack and join the rest of the human race.)

Too many parents have been duped into thinking that busy hands are happy hands. Those hands may be happy for a while. After all, kids may enjoy, even choose, gymnastics class over a family picnic. Activities are great for entertainment and to exercise bodies and minds, and they sometimes teach valuable lessons. But they don't bond you and your children together as a family unless you're *doing them together.*

Too many parents have been duped into thinking that busy hands are happy hands.

So keep an eye on how many outside-the-family individual activities your kids are involved in, because all those activities are taking away time with you. (By the way, driving your kids from activity to activity isn't considered "time" with them unless you're having much more meaningful conversations than "Hey, Shane, what do you want from McDonald's?")

That's why I recommend only one activity per child per term. When Lauren wanted to be in Brownies, that's what she did. Just Brownies. When she was in softball, that was her one activity.

If your adolescent daughter practices softball every night and travels every weekend to tournaments across the state, the odds are slim that you'll be with her when she needs a shoulder to cry on after the breakup with her boyfriend. You can't have regular, meaningful conversation if your kids are always out of the house learning how to hit a low hanging curve ball or return a backhand volley.

And here's the other thing: It's easier to coordinate time together if you have only one child, and he or she has only one activity per school term. But what if you have multiple children, and each child chooses a different activity, and all of your nights end up filled?

One family I know, who has four children ages six, eight, fourteen, and fifteen, made a decision last year to get off the wheel in their crazy scheduling. Instead of having individual music lessons (they all played different instruments), they're now involved as a family in a community band/choir that meets on Saturday afternoons, and afterward they eat take-out pizza and watch movies. It's the kids' favorite day of the week. Regarding after-school activities, the younger kids switch off picking one shared activity each semester; same thing with the older two. That means the Williams family ends up running on the activity wheel only on Tuesdays and Fridays after school, instead of the five weekdays it used to be, plus Saturdays and Sundays. On Tuesdays, everyone is home by seven o'clock for a belated dinner together. On those nights, it's Crock-Pot fare, so Mom gets to sigh with relief when the kids walk in and everyone is starving. And on Fridays? It's the one night each week that the two teenagers are allowed to schedule whatever they'd like to do with friends, starting at 7:00 p.m.

The Williams family made it a point to get off the activity wheel so they could spend more time together. With only two days of activities outside the home, both parents and the four kids happily say that their lives are a lot less stressful, and there is less sibling conflict than ever before. The family has had some amazing conversations and discovered things about one another that they'd never have known without making family dinners and discussions a priority.

You'd be amazed at the things you discover about your kids when you have unscheduled free time together. Just try it and see.

What Every Kid Needs

Activities are like ice cream. They're great for an occasional treat, but they don't make for a healthy diet. Those standing behind the counter might make you think that all your little Einstein needs is the right combination of flavors to help him construct a unified quantum theory by the time he hits puberty. But if you get on that path, you may end up ordering a cone of activities piled so high you can't possibly handle all those scoops.

What your kids need most is your love, your care, and the security of knowing where they belong. They need leisurely love, and that won't happen while you run from point A to point B.

Before your schedule gets out of hand, or if it already is, there's an easy solution: Take a meat cleaver to it. Start hacking away. Reserve the best hours and the most important days for your family. Work everything else around that. If nothing else fits, then you have your answer—you have to say no to all other options.

Meredith, a thirty-something single parent, told me recently, "The best day of my life was when I lost my BlackBerry. When I finally bought a new one a week later—hey, I'm a creature of habit—I started entering in all my family's activities. Then it hit me. *Why am I doing all this stuff?*" So she called a family counsel meeting with her three adolescent kids, and together they've been working through what few things go back in the schedule. For the first time since her divorce, Meredith and the kids are going to take a five-day vacation together and go canoeing and camping together—something they've always wanted to do.

"It's amazing how much money we've been able to save since we stopped running from activity to activity," Meredith says. Now that's a parent who's discovered what really matters—her relationship with her kids—and she's going after it. Her children will thank her down the road, if they're not already thanking her.

We all want the best for our kids—and we want our kids to be successful. But what is success to you? A perfect batting average? Winning the first violin chair? Going to the state spelling bee? Winning the regional soccer championship?

Those may all be exciting events, but do they really represent the type of true success—that feeling of affirmation and fulfillment—that carries a child for a lifetime? True success is built on self-worth—feeling good about who you are. It has nothing to do with constantly running on that little wheel—doing more and more things so you can feel accepted. It's based on strong, healthy relationships, especially with family members, and a sense of belonging that isn't based on how well you do at memorizing facts for a "Battle of the Books" event, or how well you do on your math tests, or whether you're involved in five after-school activities every week.

When Mel Brooks received a record twelve Tony Awards for his Broadway play *The Producers*, he was asked about the key to his success. His answer says everything about the priorities in his family as he was growing up: "You know, my feet never touched the floor until I was two because they were always passing me around and kissing and hugging me."[3]

What do you want your child to remember ten or twenty years from now?

Good Question!

Which activities are you currently involved in that should stay, and which should—or could—go?

Five Tips to Battle Busy

- Focus on what happens in the home, not what happens outside the home.
- Don't fall into the activity trap. Pick only one activity per semester for your child.
- Mellow out. You don't have to do everything, and neither does your child.
- Take an ax to your Day-Timer or BlackBerry. It's the best thing you could ever do for yourself.
- Slow down so your kids can take off . . . and finish well.

FOUR

MY CHILD CAN DO ANYTHING (AND OTHER MYTHS)

*Why pushing Fletcher isn't
in his (or your) best interests.*

My wife, Sande, loves the thrill of shopping. So sometimes, being the good husband I am, I go along to make her happy. On one such occasion, as I waited for her (I'm the walking shopping cart), I overheard this conversation at the mall playland:

"Look at that!" one mom said to another as her offspring evidently performed a magnificent feat. "He's so advanced for his age. He's not supposed to be able to do that for another year or so."

"Well, my Kenny could do that at fourteen months," the other mom confided. "Some kids can just do it earlier."

There was a minute of silence. I smiled because I knew what was coming next. The conversation was heating up with the "Well, my child . . ." game.

Mother number one: "My child said her first word at nine months!"

Mother number two: "Well, my child took his first steps at eight and a half months!"

Mother number three: "All my children were potty trained by eighteen months!"

Why is it that we parents have such a driving need for our kids to be number one?

Are you raising the kind of baby who wears only the latest babyGap clothes, Hanna Andersson outfits, or other expensive designer duds? Are you concerned that your child has the latest brain-stimulation toys, is developing physically faster than other kids her age, and is talking sooner as well?

Are you forcing your two-year-old, who isn't in the least interested in potty training, to potty train just because the neighbor is doing it with her two-year-old?

Does your eight-year-old have to be in Little League just because his father was—even if little David absolutely hates baseball?

Do you worry that your twelve-year-old daughter hasn't developed yet, when all the other kids in her class have?

Are you pushing your sixteen-year-old son to study harder so he can get into the best college, when all he wants to do is go to a technical school and work on cars?

Why is it that we parents think our kids can do *anything* they want to do? And why do we push them so hard?

It's because so many of us fall for the popular parenting myths. Let's continue examining these myths.

Myth No. 6: "A Gifted Child Is a Successful Child"

I talk with a lot of parents as I travel and speak around the country. And at least once on each trip I take, a parent will walk up to me after my talk, introduce him- or herself, and follow with a familiar statement: "My child is gifted."

The parent's tone seems to imply that heaven is focusing all its attention on this truly extraordinary soul, and the rest of the world should get out of the way and pay homage. It's just a matter of time until this "gifted" child gets a recording or publishing or sports contract, or a lucrative job offer from a Fortune 500 company. And, oh, by the way, the child is only six.

"Oh, I'm so sorry," I reply. "My condolences."

Inevitably, the parent stands there blinking. "W-what do you mean?" he or she stammers, stunned that anyone would treat this news with anything but enthusiasm.

That's understandable. Most people believe that a successful person is someone who has risen to the top and contributes to society. And what child is better positioned for this ascent than a gifted one, a regular little monkey when it comes to scrambling up the proverbial ladder of success?

We're all on a horizontal axis together; not one of us is better than the next person.

The truth is that we're all on a horizontal axis together; not one of us is better than the next person. I don't look down at my kids from a patriarchal top rung, for example. We need each other because we're journeying through life together. That's what being a family is all about.

But here's what most people miss. Gifts are tools; they're only as good as the one who wields them. Your son may be able to recite the value of pi to the tenth digit, but how fairly does he divide his candy with his siblings? Your daughter may be a cheerleader, homecoming queen, and valedictorian, but how well does she treat the "anonymous" girls who walk invisibly down the halls at school?

Intellect is a wonderful thing, but being smart can get your child in jail as easily as it can get him or her into MIT. (Ever hear of insider trading or computer hacking?) Being gifted without having a healthy life attitude is like a Formula One race car without much rubber left on the tires—fast in the straightaways but dangerous in the turns. Life is mostly about navigating those turns, some of them hairpin sharp.

Whether your child is gifted or not, you can prepare her for life by focusing on her attitude rather than her accomplishments.

Myth No. 7: "Starting Kids Early in School Will Give Them an Extra Edge"

Is your child a "little bluebird"?

Little bluebirds know their colors and can sing their way through the alphabet. They can count from one to ten in Spanish along with their favorite *Sesame Street* characters, and flit from word to word in their favorite book. And if that little bluebird has a fall birthday, academically it may seem to make sense to have him or her start school a year early.

Not starting kids early in school can make a tremendously positive difference in their lives, especially for boys.

Please don't.

If academics is the primary basis for starting your child early, you're probably doing him or her a disservice. Socially and emotionally, your child may not be ready. When faced with the choice of making a child the youngest or oldest kindergartener, I'll opt for the oldest nine times out of ten.

This decision won't always make a difference right away. It may not pay off until the curriculum changes significantly—in fourth grade, for example, when homework really ramps up—or when a child's body starts changing in middle school. Not starting kids early in school can make a tremendously positive difference in their lives, especially for boys.

Puberty is that time when girls may twitter about marrying the male gym teacher, while boys still relate to the female English teacher as if she's their mother. We've known for more than half a century that girls mature more quickly than boys. Giving your son that extra year for his body to grow can be a potent confidence builder when he hits the teen years, especially if he has any interest in athletics.

Notice I said "confidence builder," not "give him a better shot at making starting quarterback in the Rose Bowl." The emotional and social aspects of your child's development are much more important than whether he's first or second string *anything*. Rather than rushing him into Urchin University at age three, keep him at home to love and play with him. When school comes along, great; learning is important. But don't rush your child to grow up. It'll happen far more quickly than you'll ever imagine anyway.

Myth No. 8: "In Today's Competitive World, It's Important That a Child Finish First"

When I was twelve, I got to join the local all-star Little League team. I played third base—the "hot corner." The problem was, I wasn't so hot.

⊗ School Considerations

If you're considering starting your child in school a year early or having him or her skip a grade, ask yourself these questions:

- Am I making this decision for *myself* instead of for *my child*?
- Will sending my child to school early further crowd an already busy family activity calendar?
- Am I making this decision to allow myself or my spouse to return to work a year earlier?
- Am I considering this primarily for financial reasons?
- Am I trying to keep up with a sibling, a neighbor, a relative, or am I trying to force my child to keep up with a best friend's son or daughter?

If you answered yes to any of the above, please reconsider taking this course of action. The only thanks you receive may be the confidence you see in your child a decade down the road. But if your focus is your child's welfare and not "keeping up with the Joneses," what more encouragement do you need?

Nevertheless, I felt as if I were in heaven as our team played all-star teams from other towns. But one game was not a heavenly experience.

In the bottom of the last inning, we were up by one run with one out to go. With runners for the other team on both second and third, our coach decided to move a few players around. I switched from third base to first.

The final batter hit a grounder to my replacement at third base. As their tying run crossed home plate and their game-winning run was rounding third, the third baseman fielded the ball and fired it to me. All I had to do was catch it, and the game would be over.

I dropped the ball.

Their winning run crossed the plate. Our team lost—or, more accurately, I lost the game for us.

The other team went wild as our team watched in stunned disbelief.

I quietly began to cry.

I still remember the words echoing in my head: *Hey, stupid, all you had to do to win the game was catch the ball!*

That's a vivid memory.

But what the coach did next stands out even more vividly.

As our team slowly filed back to the third-base side, where our dugout was, my coach walked over to where I was standing. He put his arm around me and then walked with me back across the field.

"Cub," he said, using my nickname at the time, "without you we wouldn't have gotten this far."

Those words, and his arm around me, made all the difference in the world. He could have shattered me emotionally. Instead, he gave me the rare gift of confidence and perspective.

Most of us discover early on that we don't always finish first. One of the most important lessons a child can learn is how to finish *last,* how to experience and learn from failure time after time—because life is filled with it.

Unfortunately, many parents feel that their primary responsibility is to test the limits of their child's ability, to see whether he or she might be the next Shaun White or Shawn Johnson. But it's much more important to prepare our kids to live with their limitations than to give them an expectation of unbroken success.

Game-winning grand slams are not what make us who we are. What makes us who we are is how we get back into the batter's box of life after we strike out. Not having our own way or not finishing atop the dog pile of life isn't the worst thing in the world. It can teach us humility—the kind of thing your kid may need someday when he's married and has to know how to put his spouse's feelings first.

Myth No. 9: "If Children Set Their Minds to It, They Can Do Anything"

If you set your mind to it, you can accomplish a lot—that's true. But no matter how hard I try, you won't see my sixty-plus-year-old self

◈ Redefining Success

Instead of looking for the top score, consider the following:
- Did your child try hard?
- Did your child learn perseverance and the value of work?
- Is your child learning how to think, and how to be creative with the gifts she or he has been given?
- Is your child a thoughtful friend?

The answers to those questions are more important than any column of As on your child's report card or scoring the winning touchdown.

leading the four-man bobsled team at the next Winter Olympics. You *can't* do anything just because you set your mind to it.

Sounds obvious, I know. Yet the principle is easy to miss, especially when it concerns your kid. No matter how hard your child tries, he or she will never be able to reach certain goals. A good parent recognizes a child's limitations and doesn't push the child with unrealistic expectations.

For example, lots of kids love to sing and imagine themselves bopping around onstage as the latest, hottest entertainer. Yet only a few will have the voice and opportunity to succeed professionally. In fact, those who sing like me won't have a chance of making it in the church choir, much less at Madison Square Garden.

Does that mean your daughter won't *enjoy* singing? Hardly. Does that mean you shouldn't affirm her desire to sing in the school choir? Absolutely not. But it does mean she probably won't win the next *American Idol* competition or cut a platinum album. (Though having heard some of today's music, I will make exceptions to this.) If you have your mind fixed on that dream for your child, you're setting yourself—and her—up for frustration.

Sadly, many teenage girls struggle with body image and fall into anorexia nervosa and bulimia because they are trying so hard to gain the "perfect body"—like the ones they see in magazines and movies. But take a look around on your average day at the mall. How many of the people walking by have perfect bodies? Yet I've seen moms pressure teen girls into becoming models (even when the girls had no chance in the field). How much better to explain to your children that the perfect bodies they see have been shaped by hours with hair and makeup artists and trainers, countless attempts to achieve just the right camera angles, multiple photo shoots, and lots of airbrushing. Even the most gorgeous model gets a zit every once in a while. Pancake makeup can do wonders for anybody.

A good coach with a healthy perspective on life can tell whether your child has enough natural talent to go far in a given sport. Mark McGwire's dad kept him out of organized baseball until he was twelve—and then Mark hit a home run his first time at bat! Most true sports prodigies—the kind who can actually make a living at their game—show their talent early. Even if your kid is the best player in Peoria, he'll literally have to compete with the world to play professionally. Be realistic and emphasize character over skill.

In the arena of sports, look for coaches who share this view. The hyperenthusiasm of some mentors needs to be tempered with reality, especially if they're trying to live out their own dreams through their trainees. (Mmm, sounds a little like us parents, doesn't it?)

Some of the best minds in history didn't do well in school.

When it comes to academics, some children simply aren't capable of being straight-A students, no matter how hard they try. Yet many parents demand top grades from their C-level student, because without them their child can't get into the most prestigious college.

These parents worry all the time about their child's performance. They see those grades as a reflection not only of their child's worth but also of their own as well. It's important to remember that grades are simply a measure of what a student has been able to achieve in the classroom. They may not even indicate whether he or she is learning.

Some of the best minds in history didn't do well in school. School administrators thought Albert Einstein was a brick short of a full load. Can you imagine little Albert's teacher looking over his shoulder?

"Albert, Albert, what are you doing? You're supposed to be practicing your *A*s and *B*s. What is that *E*, and that little *m* and *c*? And why are you using numbers? Albert, I will be calling your mother this afternoon!"

Your IQ has little to do with whether you're going to make a difference in the world as God sees it. Love is the greatest measure.

Not every kid will be the brightest bulb on the tree.

Average Is Not a Bad Word

"My son has such potential."

"We want to help our daughter get ahead."

"We're giving our kids the opportunities we never had."

Wow. These statements sound noble, don't they? Talk about great aspirations! What parents wouldn't want to bolster their kids' confidence and watch them succeed? But if your parenting is based on these motives, you may be pushing your child for your own good rather than hers.

If your child's report card registers all As, but those grades are gained by turning the family room into night school, you might want to think again. I sometimes joke about visiting a school's science fair to search for a project that was actually done by the child himself. Most projects are done by parents who want to outdo the other parents in the classroom—and get the positive strokes that result. It's as if some moms and dads feel they're being graded themselves, and they're hoping for a report card like this to post on the refrigerator: "Mr. and Mrs. Beasley are an absolute delight to have outside class! A+++!"

But great expectations can push children too hard and too fast to do what they can't accomplish at all. And then what do you think they'll feel like? A failure. No wonder so many kids are just letting their parents drag them along through life—until they're ready to launch away from home. That's the easy way out.

So many parents start pushing their children early in life to become "above average"—as if being above average early on guarantees that little Felix or Felicia will be above average throughout life. Not so. There will always be someone who outranks little Felix or Felicia.

Here's the reality: By the time most of us hit our twenties, a few of us will be above average, a few of us will be below average, and the vast majority of us will be smack-dab in the middle. But in the end, does it really matter all that much?

Where would we be without grocery clerks, doctors, farmers, construction workers, and others? The world needs different people playing different roles.

Human development isn't a race; it's not about who gets anywhere first!

How boring it would be—and frustrating—if we were all trying to be the same and do the same jobs.

Human development isn't a race; it's not about who gets anywhere first! Character takes seasoning and really isn't seen until we're adults. I can probably drum up hundreds of kids who wanted to please the crowd—and ended up in jail.

It's so tempting, no matter what age your child is, to play the "Well, my child . . . "game. But resist it—for your own sake and especially for your child's.

Don't look around at other kids to see how your kid is doing . . . or should be doing. If you do, you're telling your child a couple of things:

1. You're not good enough.
2. You'll never be good enough.

And you're also giving away a secret best kept to yourself. Any child with normal intelligence will pick up on your tense motivation and think to himself, *Oh, I get it. Dad is really big on this. I think I'll take this on as a personal agenda!* If your life is focused on being the perfect parent who produces the perfect kids, look out. Kids have an intuitive and pretty accurate understanding of what we want them to do, and the strong-willed ones will give you a run for your money.

Oh, so Mom doesn't want to be embarrassed at lunch today, huh? I know just how to get that skateboard I've been wanting . . .

You miss so much if you get caught up in the "my child can do anything" game. Your firstborn will never be as little as she is now. I remember holding my fourth child, Hannah, who weighed five pounds two ounces at birth. She fit in one hand, and I kept saying to myself, "I catch bass this big on a routine basis!"

Perhaps because I had already raised three children into near adulthood by the time Hannah arrived (translate: I learned how to sort out my priorities and relax), I was able to enjoy her all the way around. I loved her at five pounds; I got a kick out of her at twenty-five pounds. I never stopped adoring her even when she seemed stuck at sixty pounds for two years; and I loved her at one hundred pounds. When she got married, I cried. If she has a baby someday, I know I'll love her at one hundred fifty pounds when she's nine months pregnant (although I'm sure she'll give me a swift kick in the keister if I even mention her weight then)!

Instead of comparing your kid with others, enjoy him.

Instead of comparing your kid with others, enjoy him. Like cultivating a hyacinth, plant the seed, wait awhile, keep your eyes focused on your child, enjoy the first little sprout, and then let yourself be enamored with the beauty of what ultimately comes out—twenty years down the road.

I'll never forget, when Hannah was young, pretending that the two of us were dancing at her wedding. How fast the days have raced by since then—not only with Hannah but with all my children.

I refuse to let a single memory or moment be stolen by comparing my children to their friends, or anyone else. Frankly, I don't care which friend is two inches taller, thirty seconds faster in the mile, or twenty points higher on the IQ test. Out of all the kids in the world, including famous pop stars, actresses, book authors, news anchors, you name it, I'd choose Holly, Krissy, Kevin II, Hannah, and Lauren one hundred times out of one hundred.

In the long run, what your child *can't* do doesn't matter. *Who your child is* says everything.

Good Question!

In what areas are you pushing your child beyond his or her realistic abilities? How might you adjust your expectations?

How to De-stress Your Kid's Life

- Don't play the "Well, my child . . ." game.
- Put success in its proper perspective.
- Focus on attitude over accomplishments.
- Don't rush the growing-up process.

FIVE

WHAT'S IN YOUR WALLET?

Where you spend your time and money
reveals a lot about your priorities.

Everybody wants a piece of the American dream: apple pie, Chevrolet, and . . . Disneyland.

No wonder the Walt Disney Company began airing commercials in 1987 that promoted Disneyland and Disney World after the Super Bowl. They typically featured a top NFL player answering the question, "What are you going to do next?" by shouting out, "I'm going to Disneyland!" while celebrating the team's victory right after the championship game.

Well, I don't want to pick on the Mouse too unfairly, but when you take your little kid to Disneyland at age three, buy him Mickey ears, a Goofy T-shirt, an Aladdin sword, *Lion King* pajamas, and Donald Duck sunglasses, and push your stroller the length of California, don't be surprised if at midnight you rub your sore feet and conclude that day might have been the worst of your life.

Kids don't need half as much as we give them.

Darrell was eager to give his firstborn daughter everything she wanted. One day, when picking up his daughter from a friend's house, he noticed that she loved playing with a certain musical pull toy shaped like an inchworm. Six-month-old Jessica, in fact, seemed fascinated by it.

The next day, on his way home from work, Dad went to the toy store at the mall and found the toy. What a deal! It was only twelve dollars. Even though that meant he'd have to cut down on the groceries he was also buying, Darrell bought the toy. He wanted his child to be happy.

Imagine his disappointment when he got home, took the toy out of the box, placed it on the floor, and jiggled it so it would start playing music.

What did Jessica do? She pushed right past the inchworm and started playing with the box.

"Look, Jessie," her father said. "Look at the inchworm." He jiggled the toy to get her maximum interest. "It's just like the one you saw yesterday."

But baby Jessica couldn't have cared less. She was transfixed by the box. She never even looked at the musical inchworm.

To make matters worse, Darrell's wife threw a fit about his purchase when she got home. Twelve dollars might not seem like a lot, but Darrell and his wife were on a really tight budget. Since his company was going through a big change and his hours had been cut by nearly half, his wife had taken on a part-time job just to make ends meet.

And you know how much she made an hour? Less than the toy cost.

When she found out that her husband bought the toy, do you know what she thought of first? The extra time she was going to have to be away from her baby to pay for that little inchworm or return it to the store.

All baby Jessie wanted was the box.

All she really needed was her parents' time and attention.

"Don't Make a Move! This Is a Stickup!"

Before the first television set arrived in our little western New York town back in the 1940s, radio was king. One of the most popular programs of the era was Jack Benny's comedy show. On March 28, 1948, the star aired "Your Money or Your Life," one of his most humorous—and famous—skits ever. In that episode Benny's tightwad character was mugged.

"Your money or your life!"
"I'm thinking it over."

"Don't make a move," the robber demanded. "This is a stickup!"

"Wha—?"

"You heard me!"

"Mister . . . mister, put down that gun!"

"Shut up! Now, come on. Your money or your life!"

It took only a second or two before the studio audience, recognizing the dilemma for Benny's skinflint character, began laughing.

Exasperated, the robber yelled, "Look, bud, I said, your *money* or your *life!*"

"I'm thinking it over!" Benny shot back.

Funny as this is, Benny's response captured the sad truth of how many of us act when confronted with the choice between our *money*—our houses, cars, vacations—and our *lives*—our physical and emotional well-being and our relationships with family members. It's difficult to let go of money, overly demanding jobs that will take us to the top, or richer-than-we-need lifestyles—even when the cost may be our families.

Here's a great way to find out what matters most to you. Flip through the half-hour blocks in your Day-Timer or BlackBerry or paper calendar. Then check the entries in your checkbook register. Suddenly your priorities will become very clear. If you were faced with the choice between your money or your life, would you be standing there, like Jack Benny, shouting, "I'm thinking it over!"?

Those who have a few bucks to burn usually find ways to spend them.

Designer Babies

Madonna had one. So did Sarah Jessica Parker, Celine Dion, swimsuit model Elle Macpherson, and Gwyneth Paltrow.

"It" is a Silver Cross Kensington Pram (a fancy name for a baby stroller) that retails for a mere $2,200.

My first car cost a tenth of that! And it got me more places than a baby stroller can ever go.

You can accessorize that pram with a stylish Louis Vuitton diaper bag that sells for $1,070, or a Prada version that retails for a more modest $820.

Uh, don't the parents shelling out these bucks realize what goes *in* a diaper bag?

When David Letterman finally became a dad, Madonna sent the baby a pair of Little EDA shearling baby booties. These handsewn sheepskin booties better keep those tootsies nice and toasty, since they set a person back $158—for a pair of shoes a baby probably will outgrow in two months.

If you *really* want to splurge, though, you can do what actor Chris O'Donnell did when he shelled out $4,599 for a two-story Storybook Bungalow playhouse. That playhouse costs more than the home I grew up in! Basketball star Jason Kidd outdid that: He and his wife bought a Firehouse ($5,699) and a Cotton Candy Manor ($8,299).[1]

Generally speaking, families in our Western culture are affluent. Yes, I realize that you can probably gaze up at the economic ladder and see at least a few people standing on a higher rung than yours. But if you aren't cooking your eighty-seventh variation on rice and beans, and if you have a solid roof over your head and decent clothes on your back, you're part of the upper crust of human history in terms of wealth.

Kids, of course, seldom appreciate this truth.

"Dad," my daughter Lauren asked me one afternoon when I picked her up from school, "I'm really hungry. Could we stop by Burger King?"

"Sure," I said.

We made the detour and picked up a double cheeseburger, fries, and a Frozen Cherry to boot.

"You know, Lauren," I said as we pulled out of the parking lot, "as a child I would never have *imagined* my father picking me up from school, because we walked to school."

"I know," she said between bites of cheeseburger. "Two miles."

"Exactly!" I said. "Two miles."

"Uphill, *and* in the snow, Dad," she added.

"That's right! Uphill and in the snow!"

I'm sure all of my kids got tired of hearing that story from dear old Dad, but I shared it often to make a point. That after-school trip truly would have been inconceivable to me when I was growing up. Like many families of the time, mine was poor. I remember cutting hot dogs in two to stretch the meal. My idea of high living was going to a Friday-night high-school basketball game with my parents, and then heading to a restaurant called the Colonial House for a thirty-cent hamburger and a twenty-cent hot-fudge sundae.

There's an advantage to growing up without everything your heart desires. You appreciate the little things.

But there's an advantage to growing up without everything your heart desires. You appreciate the little things.

Today, the world is a different place. Too many of us measure our worth by the years and models of our cars, the square footage and locations of our houses, the brand labels on our children's clothes. Even the hours we put into our jobs and activities serve as a gauge of success.

The problem isn't money . . . not exactly. We need food, shelter, and clothing to survive. In most of our communities, it's difficult to get by without owning a car, and it's nice to occasionally enjoy a few of the comforts of contemporary culture. The problem is our appetite for possessions and the lengths to which we'll go to better our lifestyles—often at the expense of time spent with our families.

You Get What You Pay For

When our first daughter, Holly, was eighteen months old, Sande and I went shopping for a pair of patent-leather shoes to complement Holly's beautiful red dress and white stockings. When the salesclerk found exactly what we needed, it was time to ask that question stirring deep within me, that concern encoded into male DNA: "How much are they?"

"Thirty-two dollars," replied the clerk.

My jaw dropped. Thirty-two dollars sounded like a great price for a TV back in 1974, but not for a pair of shoes. They weren't, after all, real ruby slippers. At that point the shoes came flying off Holly faster than you could click your heels together and say, "There's no place like home."

I suppose we could have stretched our budget, bought the shoes, and worked a bit harder to pay them off. But spending more time at the office to afford patent-leather shoes—or a more luxurious car or house, for that matter—wasn't what we valued then, and it isn't what we value now.

Given the choice between patent-leather shoes and more leisurely time together at home with my children, I'll choose time together any day.

Those shoes are simply one small example of how every decision you make comes with a price tag. The financial bottom line is only the beginning and often isn't even the most costly. If you trade homegrown kids for store-bought goods, you'll get what you pay for—which may include a family living on leftover scraps of your time and energy.

Every decision you make comes with a price tag.

What's the "Real Cost"?

When you drop twelve hundred dollars on the sporting-goods-store counter for a new set of golf clubs, that may seem like a great deal. But you aren't simply dropping hundreds of dollars from your recreation budget. You're declaring your intention to spend time swinging those clubs with friends, work colleagues, and clients. You're buying into Thursday evenings at the driving range and Friday mornings and Saturday afternoons on the back nine.

What's the real cost? Perhaps twelve hundred dollars plus two hundred hours per year, which equals who knows how many missed opportunities as your children grow up.

Eighteen years may seem like an eternity. But if your child is six years old, you're already one-third of the way through the time you have to raise her. If she's nine, half your days together have passed. Time really does fly when you're out having fun. If you aren't careful, those years when your child most wants to spend time with you will fly by faster than a golf ball careening off a titanium driver.

I know a young middle-school assistant principal who takes this challenge seriously. Now nearing forty, he's decided he wants to run marathons. (Why anybody would want to do anything quite so stupid as running twenty-six miles without stopping is beyond me. If I want pain like that, I'll just hand you a two-by-four and tell you to whack me over the head. One look at my figure, and you'll know why I say that. My own marathon is more likely grazing on a slice—or two or three—of Marie Callender's pumpkin pie while sitting in my own kitchen.)

Since training for a marathon requires many hours, and his kids are young, I asked him, "When do you do the long runs?"

"It's kind of embarrassing," he answered.

"Go on—tell me."

"I wake up at 3:20 a.m. and run before work."

"So it's dark the entire time you're running?"

"Yeah. I have a headlight. You see, there's no way I can come home from work at 5:00 p.m. and tell my kids, 'Sorry, but Daddy has to leave for another hour and a half.' If I want to run, I have to do it before work."

"When do you sleep?"

"I go to bed when my kids do. It might seem kind of silly, a grown man going to bed at nine o'clock, but that's what works best for my family."

Life is all about looking at the real cost—the way we spend our money, the way we spend our time.

It's not silly at all. In fact, I think it's wonderfully refreshing. This man so values his home and his family that rather than attempting to bend his family around his hobby, he's willing to bend his hobby around his growing family.

You see, life is all about looking at the real cost—the way we spend our money, the way we spend our time. Hunting or fishing or hiking or gaming may provide enjoyment for you and your friends, and everybody deserves a break here and there. But the smart parent, like that assistant principal, knows that those hours need to be balanced with plenty of time with your spouse and children.

If you, like many folks, are more materially minded than activity prone, you'll need to be extra careful. You know that new house with the bigger yard you just "have" to have? Ever thought about the time required to clean those extra rooms and maintain that yard? Yeah, you can hire a cleaning lady or a landscaper, but then you'll have another two regular monthly expenses requiring you to bring in even more income.

The same principle applies when you purchase that new car on credit. I've heard of families with an annual income of fifty thousand dollars buying a new minivan for twenty-five thousand. They don't have the cash up front, so after they make the interest payments (at least another ten thousand dollars) and cover the taxes and licenses and all that stuff, they've spent almost an entire year's income to buy one vehicle! Do you really want to spend eight hours a day, five days a week, away from your family for nine or ten months just so you can buy a brand-new vehicle? Is that *really* a good trade?

There's no law that says you need a new minivan—or a new garage shed—just because other families are getting them. And what's more important in the long run—one-upping your neighbors' purchases or seeing a smile on your son's face when you set up a tent in your backyard and sleep there overnight to look at the stars? Bet you anything those neighbors would rather be doing what you're doing than wading through the extra bills every month.

Money can buy many things, but there are two important things it can never buy: happiness and lifelong relationships. Those two "gold" items will keep their value far longer than anything that will wear out or rust.

What You're Doing Shouts So Loudly, I Can't Hear What You're Saying!

Did you know that your actions *always* speak louder than your words? In fact, they not only speak, they shout *over* your words? The attitudes you hold toward possessions, time, and money strongly influence how your kids will view those things.

⊗ Be a Smart Shopper!

- Shop only for the items you and your family truly need. Make a list before you go to the store or shop online.
- Evaluate all purchases before you buy them. For larger purchases, research prices and make notes first. Then walk away from your purchase for a few days. After the glow of a potential purchase wears off, you'll be amazed at the money you save by not buying the items you decide you don't need.
- Think through the time and commitment any new purchases will require (e.g., the famous home gym that gets used for a week and then becomes an expensive coatrack).
- Above all, don't shop just to have something to do.

What does your current lifestyle say about your view toward money?

Have you ever heard the catchy saying from the 1980s: "He who dies with the most toys wins"?

But wins what? I have to ask. More toys to pile on your grave?

Not many people ask from their deathbeds, "Would everyone please excuse us for a moment? I want a few minutes alone with my jewelry." No one asks to hold that set of golf clubs one last time, or for one final glimpse at his waxed and polished Lexus. Material possessions don't hold bedside vigils when your end is near; they can't cry with you in your pain, or laugh at shared stories.

I mention this because families with "bucks to burn" may be at a higher risk of misplacing priorities simply because they can afford it. When you have significant discretionary income, you have temptations galore. Paul, a wise man from long ago, said that "the love of money is a root of all kinds of evil" (1 Timothy 6:10). And he was right.

But note that he didn't say *money* is evil; he said that the *love of money* is the problem. Everyone needs some money to survive—to buy food and provide lodging and clothing. It's when money becomes something we love and use to fulfill other needs in life—such as our need for love and relationships—that it becomes a hothouse of trouble.

The temptations seem harmless enough. You may have the means for your child to pursue any activity that suits your fancy, from preschool French tutorials to gymnastics class three times a week for your eighteen-month-old to Suzuki violin lessons with a master teacher for your four-year-old.

Is it any wonder that scenarios like the following happen on a regular basis, especially in middle-class or more affluent areas?

> A shocked mother overheard a visiting friend tell her son, "Man, you must really be poor. You don't even have an upstairs or a basement."
>
> A ten-year-old girl had a friend over for a day. Toward the end of the day, they were tired and decided to watch a movie. After a while, though, the friend threw up her arms in disgust and said, "I'm going home. I can't stand to watch this. It's just not a big-screen TV!" With that, she called her mother and asked her to come pick her up.

Kids are shaped by the environment their parents establish. If yours know only privilege, they'll have little patience for "sacrificing" by watching a twenty-seven-inch television and won't even think about how rude it is to get up and walk away.

Your actions really do speak louder than words. How do you

respond when your three-year-old accidentally spills her strawberry milkshake all over the interior of your brand-new car? Or what about when your sixteen-year-old has a fender bender with that same car two days later?

How you feel about your money will also speak volumes to your kids about how valuable they are, compared to how you treat your possessions.

Should Your Kid Work?

Modeling a balanced, disciplined work ethic will teach your kids by example. But what about after-school jobs? Aren't they also necessary to get children ready for the "real" world?

Many parents encourage their high schoolers to work outside the home to help pay for clothes, games, trips, and college. These parents want to teach their children the value of money and the discipline of hard work. But I believe there are more important things during the school year for sixteen-year-olds to be focusing on: schoolwork, housework, friendships, and time with family.

The day will come soon enough for working outside the home. In the meantime, kids can learn the value of money by helping to write the checks for family bills and managing an allowance. I understand the economic realities many families face today and realize that many kids need to work during summers to help pay for college and other expenses. But during the school year, most kids have enough going on without jumping into a year-round job.

Look at it this way: Sande and I could have allowed Hannah to flip burgers and earn six dollars an hour working five-hour shifts, for a paltry thirty dollars. Or, in lieu of that, we could spend an afternoon together as a family—perhaps watching a movie, going for a walk or drive, getting ice cream, or even staying home and cleaning the house or cooking dinner together. At the end of that day, would I even consider trading that family time for thirty bucks?

Not a chance.

Does Time Equal Money?

The saying "time is money" may be true in business, but when it comes to family life, time isn't simply as good as gold; it's better. You may charge clients two hundred dollars per hour at the office, but the value of that hour spent with your children is priceless.

The best thing you can give your kids is not the dirt bike, the brand-name clothes, the new car at sixteen. What they want and need is your *time*. Time to play together. To laugh together. Time to listen to their struggles and questions. Time simply to do life together.

Rich or poor, we're all given the same amount of time each day. You can't buy more. You can't even really save it. You can only spend it differently.

The question is, how will you spend those twenty-four hours each day? How much will you invest in what lasts for a lifetime—your family?

One day I'd just arrived home on a flight from New York to Tucson and was still feeling as if someone had run me through our dryer's permanent-press cycle.

"Dad, can you drive me down to Walgreens?" Hannah asked.

"What's at Walgreens?" I responded.

"I need supplies for school."

"Sure, I'll drive you down."

I was jet-lagged, but I wanted to see my daughter more than I wanted to see my pillow. She'd been working at camp all summer; I'd been in New York for a few days. And how often does a father get time with his daughter?

You don't have to look far to find mindless clutter to occupy your time: junk mail, games on your cell phone, reality television.

Why not take advantage of unanticipated opportunities with your kids? Why not take advantage of *unanticipated* opportunities with your kids instead? When you're in the car together, will you choose to switch on talk radio or strike up a conversation of your own? When you're sitting at the breakfast table, will you pick up the newspaper or get the latest scoop from your child? On a Sunday afternoon, will you tune in the game on the tube or tune in to your child and go outside to toss a ball around?

The question isn't so much "How often do I get to be with my child?" as it is "How often do I make the best of our moments together?" Most of these moments are free—or at least inexpensive. When I drove my ninety-four-year-old mother back to the nursing home after a visit, I asked Lauren if she wanted to come along. She did.

"Mom," I asked, "would you like to stop and get an ice cream? Lauren, how about you?"

The council convened, the vote was unanimous, and we made the detour to enjoy a little extra time together.

Most of life is composed of such mundane activities: grocery shopping, dropping off and picking up the kids from school, swinging by the bank drive-through, doing dishes after dinner. But it's easy to forget, in the flurry of things, why we're doing them: It's all for our traveling companions in the minivan of life.

Those special, spontaneous moments can do far more for our children than shelling out $5,000 for a weeklong vacation at Disneyland, where you'll stand in line, pay $3.50 for a small ice-cream sandwich, and come home cranky and tired. Resist the allure of brand-name clothing, the latest cars, the biggest house the bank will let you mortgage, and the hot-spot vacation destinations. All these things should take a backseat to spending time with the ones you love.

Kids will get tired of most toys. In fact, toys last just about as long as leftovers—kids lose interest in them faster than you can believe. As soon as you buy one video game, the next newer, better video game is out. So don't give your kids what they want; give them what they need.

Your kids don't need more stuff. They need you. And the more things a kid has, the less time he or she usually spends with Mom and Dad.

So focus on what's lasting. Don't give your kids things to replace their time with you. Instead, let them experience life *with* you.

Good Question!

Before you buy something, ask yourself, Do I need it, or do I simply want it? And what's the *real cost* of that item—in money, time, and relationships?

Price: $0.00

- Hearing two-year-old's laughter when you blow dandelions at each other.
- Enjoying a grilled-cheese-sandwich picnic in the backyard.
- Appreciating twenty-four hours in a day.
- Walking your neighbor's dog.
- Hosting a campout in your basement.
- Raking a big pile of fall leaves—and jumping in it!

SIX

IT'S NOT WHAT YOU DO; IT'S WHO YOU ARE

How to raise kids from the inside out.

Michael Young wasn't your ordinary homecoming king. He didn't have a throwing arm to lead the football team to a state championship. He didn't have the athletic body to make girls twitter in the hallways. While others solved physics problems, Michael took life-skills classes and had a hard time adding two and two.

An eighteen-year-old senior at Jefferson High School in Bloomington, Minnesota, Michael may have been developmentally delayed in math, social studies, and science. But his attitude was truly gifted.

Michael studied school yearbook photos until he knew each of the seventeen hundred students by name. He served as student manager of the basketball team and rarely missed a school sporting event. Before bed each night, he listened to a CD of the Jefferson band.

He's as selfless an eighteen-year-old as you'll find; running for homecoming king wasn't even his idea. Drew Glowa, senior class president and captain of the hockey team, talked him into it. Drew got the seventy-five names needed on Michael's petition and campaigned for him—even though Drew was running for homecoming king himself.

Not surprisingly, Michael's family has had much to do with his outlook on life. Those who know Michael's parents and his older sister, Laura, say they're all "positive, so giving, so dogged in opening doors for Michael."

The thought of losing the election didn't faze Michael. In fact, he told his parents on the way to school that day that he hadn't even voted for himself. But when he found out that his fellow students had chosen him to be homecoming king, he was ecstatic. He ran around the gym, nearly dragging the homecoming queen, giving high fives all around, and wearing a grin as big as his heart.[1]

Mr. and Mrs. Young obviously did something right to raise a boy to be so positive, giving, support-ive of fellow students, and enthusiastic about life—even though he faced spe-cial challenges. Cultivating character like Michael's takes work, but oh the benefits it reaps for a lifetime for every-one around him. Seventeen hundred students watched Michael respond with joy and passion to his "mis-sion" of being the homecoming king. It's a day that all of Jefferson High will remember with misty eyes.

Who you are is so much more important than what you can do, what you own, or how you look.

Michael was a walking, running, and leaping example that day to everyone, illustrating that who you are—your character, the way you relate to people and respond to the curves life throws at you—is so much more important than what you can do, what you own, or how you look.

And his parents were right behind him, cheering him on all the way.

Straight to the Heart

Have you ever seen the movie *Searching for Bobby Fischer*?[2] If not, it's one of the few movies worth your time. Based on the true story of a young chess prodigy named Josh Waitzkin, it clearly reveals how a parent can influence a child's mental and emotional development.

"You have a good heart," his mother tells him one night as she tucks him in, "and that's the most important thing in the world."

But later in the movie, the night before an important chess tournament, Josh's performance-obsessed father tucks his boy into bed with the words, "You won't lose, Josh."

"What if I do?" Josh speculates.

"You won't!"

"I'm afraid I might."

"Josh, they're afraid. They're terrified of you. Now you get some sleep."

"Maybe it's better not to be the best," Josh suggests. "Then you can lose and it's okay."

Which of those tuck-ins do you think helped Josh have a good night's sleep? The one that acknowledged the importance of Josh's heart.

It's so easy, though, to focus only on what's on the surface, isn't it?

"Do you have a girlfriend yet?" we ask our six-year-old nephew.

"You look so pretty!" we coo at the neighbor's eighteen-month-old girl.

"Oh, I bet you'll grow up to be an engineer," we say to our child as he tinkers with his tricycle.

Why does the heart so often get missed?

We're too quick to admire the throwing arm of a future NFL quarterback, the shrewdness of a someday CFO, the confident strut of tomorrow's pop singer. But without character, that future quarterback may be settling a lawsuit over a sexual-harassment charge from his college days. That CFO may be jailed because he doctored the books, losing millions of investors billions of dollars. And that pop star? She may have such a low view of marriage that she gets hitched and then has the marriage annulled in less than three days.

"Beauty is only skin deep," the saying goes. But true beauty, the kind that lasts long after the body begins to sag, goes clear to the heart. And it all starts with how you, as a parent, imprint character on your child's heart.

Imprinting Your Child's Character

In her book *Home by Choice: Raising Emotionally Secure Children in an Insecure World*, Dr. Brenda Hunter, psychologist and author, describes what I call the "indelible imprint" that a parent leaves on a child. She believes that the parental relationship forms the basis for a child's perceptions of himself or herself:

> According to [John] Bowlby, a young child forms "internal working models" of himself, his parental attachments, and his world out of the raw material of his parental relationships. Based on the way his parents treat him, a child will form certain expectations about how others will treat him. If the parents are warm, loving, and emotionally accessible, the child comes to believe that *he* is loving and worthy. As he matures, he will possess high self-esteem; he will be able to trust others and, later in life, have the capacity to be intimate with a spouse and children. Secure in his parental attachments, this individual will expect others to treat him the same way his parents have.[3]

What makes an indelible imprint on your child? Your physical affection, your presence at home, and your spoken words. If your child hears "you don't amount to much," she'll come to believe what she hears. But if your child hears consistent affirmations that she is loved, she'll form a mental image of herself that fits those messages. And loved children who know they are loved become children and adults who can reach out in love to others.

When our daughter Hannah entered her junior year of high school, four foreign-exchange students from Germany were about to experience their first day in a U.S. classroom. Sande and I encouraged Hannah to go out of her way to make the German kids feel welcomed. We wanted her to empathize with those kids, being in a strange place, with new families, and among strangers whose language was different.

"Imagine if you were starting school today in Germany," I told Hannah. "How would you want others to treat you? You can do what you want, but here's what I think might be good. Go up to those kids and not only meet and welcome them, but then go back

How to Create a Giver . . . Not a Taker

- Teach your child not only to say thank you but also to write thank-you notes. Even a birthday present from Grandma isn't a "right"; it's a privilege and should be treated as such.
- Involve your child in your acts of charity. If you know of a family who could use some grocery money, write a card, put the cash inside, and have your child walk it to the other family's door. It's a great way to model your own concern for others.
- Sponsor a child in another country. As a family, we Lemans sponsor a boy in El Salvador through Compassion International. Lauren loves to write letters to him. In addition to regular support, we like to get creative. One time I went to a flea market and purchased a bunch of baseball bats, baseball gloves, and numerous balls, enough for the whole neighborhood in El Salvador to play baseball! Lauren played a part in finding and purchasing the equipment, as well as packing and mailing the package.

It comes down to this: If you want to raise a compassionate child, then give him or her something to be compassionate about.

at least a second time to each of them, reminding them what your name is and telling them that if there's anything they don't understand or need help with, just look for Hannah."

Why did we encourage our daughter to step outside her comfort zone? Because to us the most important part of a child's development is her character.

At the end of that first day of her junior year, I was interested in hearing from Hannah more than how she liked her teachers and classes. I wanted to know whether she talked to those four kids. You see, when it comes to my children's education, I care more about their servant hearts than their performance in math.

Feeling Good or Having Self-Worth?

"Oh, Johnny, you're so marvelous! Look at you go!"

"You're just the best, Karen!"

Let's give kids some credit. They're not as stupid as we think they are. When you tell a kid how wonderful he is, and he knows he's not wonderful, how do you think that settles in his mind? *Uh-huh, that's a good one. Mom and Dad are lying again.* The only thing this kind of feel-good therapy accomplishes is telling your child that he can't trust you. Then if he ever does accomplish something worthwhile, and you give him a genuine compliment, he won't believe you. *Mom and Dad are just lying again,* he'll think.

Today, so many parents are concerned that their kids have good self-esteem, they bend over backward to help them get it. But kids know that meaningless compliments are nothing but blue smoke adults blow their way. One father told me the other day that his young daughter called the "participant" ribbons handed out at a track meet "Good job anyway" ribbons. She quickly tired of these meaningless strips, and rightly so. It's an accomplishment to finish a marathon; it's not a particular accomplishment for a ten-year-old to finish a fifty-meter dash (except at the Special Olympics or similar events, of course).

True self-worth isn't just feeling good about yourself. It comes from accomplishing something and from giving something back to others.

Let's say your child works very, very hard to understand decimals. Math has never been her forte, but she's determined to spend extra time each night trying to understand decimals. The next week, she comes home with a B on her math test. Then it's time to celebrate! Why wait for that A? Come alongside your child, celebrate her hard work, comment on what a great job she did and how proud you are of her for sticking to her task.

"Honey, doesn't it feel good to work hard and accomplish your goal? Wow, a B! That's just terrific! Hey, let's put that paper on the fridge and surprise Daddy when he gets home, shall we?"

Such conversations and actions are what build a child's character and self-worth. Your child starts thinking to herself, *Wow. The most significant people in my life—my mommy and my daddy—notice the work I've done and what I've accomplished. And they're proud of me!*

How can you build true, healthy self-worth in children? Encourage their good thinking. Point out what they're doing right.

No, your child didn't get an A and will probably never get an A in math. But when a C math student works hard and pulls off a B, that's a significant accomplishment and should be celebrated!

Such compliments, built on substance—actual work done and goals accomplished—go a long way in building your child's character for a lifetime.

Though I'm not big on filling a child's schedule with activities, what I love about a club like 4-H is that a kid will take on a project—raising a calf, for instance—and learn to see the project through from square one. At the end, if he does a good job, he gets the blue ribbon at the fair—and he's earned it! That sense of accomplishment and pride is a good thing, because it's based on substantive reality. The child didn't just try hard—he succeeded. In the real world, that's a significant difference and a very important distinction.

True encouragement means recognizing what a child does and acknowledging her actual accomplishments, whether those accomplishments take place in school or at home. It's about noticing those things that deserve to be noticed, and taking the time to mention them.

How can you build true, healthy self-worth in children? Encourage their good thinking. Point out what they're doing right. Notice the choices and actions that are worthy of encouragement, and don't be sparing. Shelve the empty rah-rah, "you're special because you're you" stuff.

Ten Ways to Rear a Kid from the Inside Out

If you want to raise a child who has character—a good heart, decent manners, consideration, patience, and forgiveness—rather than one who *is* a character, try the following ten ways to rear a child from the inside out.

1. Understand Your Child's Uniqueness

I always enjoy observing the ducks that congregate at the edge of the lake outside our house. And when they waddle, honking, onto the grass, I feed them cracked corn.

But you want to know what amazes me the most? Even with a lake full of ducklings that look all the same to me, every mother duck somehow seems to know her own.

I guess every duckling is different. I *know* every human is.

When your child was born or adopted, you began unraveling the mystery of his or her uniqueness. For some of you, the process began as you learned the sex of your baby when the doctor turned that newborn over and checked out the plumbing. You watched to see whether the baby's personality was as tranquil as a pond or as active as a mountain waterfall. You listened and learned to discern whether your baby was crying because of hunger, loneliness, fear, or simply needed a poopy diaper changed.

> **The beauty of your relationship is that there's never been another quite like it.**

As your child grows, you discover whether his favorite book is *Curious George* or *The Little Engine That Could*. Later you notice whether he likes rap or jazz. You shake your head as he grows up loving astrophysics and then in college switches to creative writing, or as he transforms from being quiet as a whisper to being outspoken and determined in politics.

The beauty of your relationship is that there's never been another quite like it. You'll always uncover new things about yourself and your child as you spend time together. These are the "quiet" discoveries of family life, more exciting and fulfilling than anything Lewis and Clark, Christopher Columbus, or a NASA astronaut ever witnessed. Don't miss them by keeping yourself and your kids running on the activity wheel. It's time to get off that wheel and onto the solid ground of relationships that last a lifetime.

2. Give Your Kids a Piece of You

In at least one respect, dogs and kids are pretty much alike.

No matter where I am in the house, our dog, Rosie, insists on following me more closely than a tick. She not only sits next to me; she insists on sitting *on* me. She's a lapdog, a little cocker spaniel. She'll come bounding up with her squeaky toy, dripping saliva, and drop it right on my clean pants.

Here's the strong similarity between Rosie and my kids: All of them want a piece of me. Squeaky toys, doggie biscuits, even tenderloin steaks may satisfy for a while, but they'll never replace me. Yet

What your kids want more than anything is a piece of you.

kids and pets will take what they can get. If you allow the relationship to become about giving them car rides, buying them new video games, and just keeping them busy, they'll take that.

But what your kids want more than anything is a piece of you. A good, healthy piece. Not the leftovers you can scrape up after you've doled out your time and talents and emotional energies to everyone else.

If you doubt that your child really wants to spend time with you, just ask any child whose parent took her out on "dates" whether she remembers details from those one-on-one outings. You're sure to get some stories. Brenda, one of five siblings, remembers sweating through a thirteen-mile bike ride in the Florida sun with her father, but she relished it nevertheless, because just the two of them were together. Frank, an only child, remembers getting lost on a hike with his dad in the Rockies when he was just six years old. It was a bit scary at first, but those hours created a lifelong memory he'll cherish forever.

Laura, now thirty, remembers her dad faithfully taking her to a horse farm each Saturday morning when she was a child. As she rode her favorite horse, he'd shovel horse manure and clean out stalls in exchange for her lesson. But his eyes and heart were always with his daughter, and she knew it. On the way home, he'd always tell her about a skill of hers he could see developing—and they'd talk about it at home over fried eggs and hot chocolate. To this day, just a whiff of fried eggs or steaming hot chocolate reminds her of that special time with her father.

3. Treat Each Child Differently

I once listened to four adult siblings talk among themselves after the funeral of one of their parents. Each eagerly recounted all that the deceased parent had done with him or her individually. Each had secretly thought his or her relationship with that parent was the most special in the family. All were shocked to discover that their brothers and sisters had the same thought. What a wonderful gift and legacy that parent left to each child!

There's no such thing as one-size-fits-all parenting. So don't even try. Every child is unique, and that means your relationship with each child is unique, and uniquely suited to your personalities.

Some kids learn character best by verbal instruction; some learn by tactile involvement; others learn by seeing an example. Some are incredibly sensitive and need only an eyebrow raised in discipline (like Carmen, who could never even take an extra cookie out of the cookie jar without confessing to her mother). Others need a firmer approach (like her sister, Morgan, who could be a poster child for Dr. Dobson's book *The Strong-Willed Child*).

Kids thrive on the special connections that grow from your unique relationship with them.

Kids thrive on the special connections that grow from your unique relationship with them. When Hannah and Lauren were younger, I called them by nicknames. Lauren was "my little muffin," and Hannah was "my little peanut." They ate up this "muffin" and "peanut" talk, because for each of them, it created a unique connection with me.

I must have gotten my food groups mixed up one day, though. In a disastrous slip of the tongue, I called Lauren "my little peanut" and Hannah "my little muffin." Boy, did they ever make me eat those words! I found out just how passionately they held to their special distinctions. In their minds, the mix-up was a great betrayal, like forgetting an anniversary or the details of a first date with a spouse.

To my kids, and to yours, those customized connections are markers of intimacy, so form them, and use them, with great care.

4. Give Your Kids Rituals

When our older kids were growing up, Friday mornings meant treats from the bakery. There were all sorts of goodies to choose from, which made it hard for me to decide between the turnovers, the raspberry-filled doughnuts, and the maple bars. But Krissy never had a problem with her order; she always asked for a little petit four. She requested it so regularly that it became a ritual between us.

When that tiny pastry came out of the box at home every Friday, it wasn't only the thought of how good it would taste that pleased her. It was also the fact that I'd been thinking of her when she wasn't around. When someone does something nice for you in your absence, that's a pretty good sign you hold a cherished place in that other person's life.

When I brought that petit four home each week, Krissy also felt loved because she saw that I knew her and her preferences. Of course, simply knowing a list of things your child likes isn't enough.

Kids thrive on the right kind of rituals.

You may know he likes baseball and may pick him up a Yankees baseball cap on your way through LaGuardia during a New York business trip. But if you never throw a baseball with him or attend his games, then that cap won't mean much, because it doesn't point back to a shared life.

Kids thrive on the right kind of rituals. A review of studies (thirty-two of them, to be exact) from the past half century backs this homegrown approach: Family routines and rituals are "important to the health and well-being of today's busy families."[4]

Rituals often get their start without planning. Maybe you did something once that your child loved, which you've repeated until it became a routine. Your boys may have been building a fort out of sofa cushions late one afternoon when you came home from work, and you decided to initiate a wrestling match. Now your sons build their forts and strategize every afternoon at 4:45 p.m., waiting for your return so they can put you in a headlock.

Keep your eyes open for the next ritual you can establish—the next thing your kids latch on to, an interaction that meets their needs and builds your homegrown bond.

5. Put Your Relationship with Your Kids First

Raising kids and "making them mind" is a lot easier than any of us make it out to be. It all comes down to one simple thing—the relationship you have with them.

If your children feel they belong to your family, they have little reason from a psychological standpoint to act out. And they have good reason to listen when you try to cultivate their character. So instead of trying too hard to help your children get ahead in life, help them get to know you.

The authoritarian parent who says, "I'm the parent, and you're going to do what I tell you to do!" isn't too interested in the relationship. Instead, he cares about getting the job done, and done well. Sadly, the authoritarian parent often raises children just like himself, who can't bond with a husband or wife and don't know how to give of themselves to their own children.

The laissez-faire parent who acts on the "Hey, anything goes. Let's just all get along, shall we?" principle isn't too interested in the relationship either. She's just interested in not making waves. (And, boy, do her kids know how to work her. After all, since happiness is her primary goal, those kids have pulling at her heartstrings down pat. They play the sob-story violin for all it's worth . . . because ninety-nine times out of one hundred, it works.) Sad to say, such children often end up as self-centered adults who are takers rather than givers in their relationships.

But when you put your relationship with your child before his performance, you're preparing him from the inside out. He takes his cues from the way you interact with him: If you're disappointed, he feels that and adjusts accordingly. If you're pleased, he knows he's on the right track and thrives.

Such feedback leads to character development. Encourage this process by building a solid relationship in which your kids know that you know them, love them, and even *like* them.

6. Be Real

One day, eleven-year-old Lauren and I were in the pool, floating on our blow-up plastic pool toy. At that time Lauren was very conscious that her body was starting to change—and knew that her swimsuit showed the changes. Wanting her to know that she wasn't the only one who'd faced embarrassment, I brought up my own pubescent experience in swimming class—which I would have done *anything* to get out of.

"When Daddy was in seventh and eighth grade," I said, "we had to swim in the nude during swimming class."

"What?" Lauren asked, shocked.

"We didn't have swimming suits," I replied.

"You mean you went in . . . *bare?*" she asked. Her eyes were as huge as silver dollars.

"Yeah."

She blinked. "What was that like?"

"It was terrible," I replied. "I had to sit on the edge of the pool with all the other boys in my gym class—probably thirty or so— while the teachers took attendance. Then we were in the pool for a fifty-minute period, and the teachers were sticklers about making you do it."

When I shared that story, somehow a bathing suit didn't seem all that skimpy to Lauren anymore.

Sometimes parenting involves sharing some pretty painful memories. When those times come, be real with your kids: Share the uncertainty, the regret, and even your own mistakes. It doesn't mean you have to tell them everything about your past—what has happened to you and the dumb things you did. But leveling the playing field between you and your kids will help them wrestle through their own difficult times.

Your children will discover you're not perfect if they haven't already, so get real. Drop the facade.

Cultivating character doesn't mean faking it. Your children will discover you're not perfect if they haven't already, so get real. Drop the facade. Standing in for God might be a much more enjoyable role to play, especially if you're ashamed of the times you were mischievous or dishonest. But hiding those incidents won't help your children deal with their own imperfections.

Talk about your downs as well as your ups. I don't mean sharing sordid details. But as you communicate that you, too, have experienced problems in life, that will help your children know they're not alone.

Maintaining a godlike persona will only distance your children as they realize they're made of mortal stuff. The essence of developing intimacy with your kids is telling them who you really are and giving them the opportunity to tell you who they really are.

I'm not talking about trying to be your child's best buddy. He or she needs your parental experience and wisdom. But talking with your kids about uncomfortable subjects as naturally as you can will help them find comfort in discussing subjects *they* feel uncomfortable about.

7. Nurture Your Child's Trust

If your child opens her heart and tells you something confidential, don't run over it or make fun of it. If she tells you that she doesn't feel she fits in at school, don't dismiss it by saying, "Honey, you shouldn't worry about that!" If your son asks, "Dad, what's a condom?" don't strike down the question by saying, "We don't talk about things like that!" Take these confidences in stride; hear your child out; take his or her heart seriously.

Your child's vulnerability is a sign of intimacy. So don't brush it aside or, worse, belittle it. Take the vulnerable moments as a gift—the gift of a growing relationship, which is a prerequisite for building character.

8. Model Values Worth Catching

I was in line to grab a burger at the local Wendy's. The son of the man in front of me walked over from the table where the rest of the family sat. I couldn't hear the little boy's question, but I had no problem hearing the father's response.

"Well, you tell your mother that if she wants something, she can just come over and get it!" he snapped.

I wondered, *What kind of husband is that little boy going to be someday? How will he treat women? When his wife asks him if he'll bring napkins from the kitchen, will he follow what his daddy taught him?*

I ordered my meal, glad that my children weren't there to hear the man's outburst. Had they been, I would have said to them, "There are people in life who talk like that, people who disrespect their kids and their spouses by screaming at them. Your job is to find someone who is not like that."

Values are caught, not taught. Your kids are watching your every move, taking mental notes. The beliefs and behavior you model are the foundation on which your children's character is built. The way you see your children is the way they'll see themselves.

Your kids are watching your every move, taking mental notes.

If you respect your kids, they'll see themselves as respectable. If you are gracious with them, they'll learn grace themselves. If you listen to them, they'll grow up listening to others and believing they have a voice worth hearing.

9. Use Chores to Teach Character and Responsibility

My wife, Sande, once threw a banana peel on the kitchen floor and left it there to see what the rest of us would do. One by one, our kids walked by and looked at it. *Oh,* you can imagine them thinking, *someone's getting in trouble.*

Later that day Sande asked, with a magnificently uplifted eyebrow (she does that so well), "Did anyone notice the banana peel on the kitchen floor? I know you all walked by it."

You tell them, Sande, I thought. *What were you thinking, kids? I thought we taught you better than that.*

"But *you,*" she said, turning to me, "*you* looked at it, kicked it aside with your foot, and kept right on going."

Oh.

I got in *big* trouble that time, the psychologist failing the psychology experiment. Apparently, through my own example, I *hadn't* taught my children better than that.

Most of us, parent and child alike, have thought at one time or another, *That's not my job.* And sometimes it's not. But I'm always pleased to see customers in the grocery store picking up cereal boxes that have tipped off the shelves or apples that have rolled to the produce-section floor. When I see an accident like that, I stop to help.

⊗ Chores, Anyone?

Chores are a good way to teach character . . . with a few caveats:

- Make jobs age appropriate. Don't ask your four-year-old to hand-wash your crystal, and then scream when he or she drops an expensive piece.
- To avoid conflict between siblings (e.g., Fletcher cleaning the toilet and Veronica cleaning the bathroom sink), have kids work in different areas of the house.
- Change the jobs occasionally. There's nothing worse than being "the garbage person" for life . . . with no hope of parole.
- If you want a job done right, do it yourself—but I'm talking about parenting, not sweeping the floor. If you want to teach your two-year-old daughter to pitch in, give her a broom and dustpan and a lot of slack. Don't stand over her like a field marshal and criticize her work. For kids ages two to four, it's much more important that they learn enthusiasm for helping than make the kitchen floor sparkle.

If the kids are with me, they learn more about chipping in than they would from any lecture I could ever give them about helping out around the house. (I can guarantee that no one in the Leman house has ever forgotten Sande's banana-peel experiment either.)

10. Look Out for Others

"Why do you stop at stop signs?" I often ask people.

Most will answer, "So I don't get in an accident."

Others may say, "It's the law."

Those are pretty good reasons. But I hope we also stop at stop signs so that we don't hurt other people.

It's easy to start with "Number One" and move outward from

there. But what a wonderful gift when you can instill in your child a heart that looks out for others *first*.

To cultivate selflessness, enlist your family's participation. If a storm lashes the neighborhood and scatters debris over the yard, don't ask the kids, "Would you like to help Mommy?" Given the choice of picking up the yard or playing with a friend, you're not going to hear, "Oh, really, can we, Mom?" Most kids aren't waiting eagerly for a cue to help; after all, they're hedonistic me-me-ers at heart. Until they're taught to think of others, it won't come naturally. Your children need *gentle* direction until they learn over time that pitching in is expected.

"Come on, everybody to the backyard. We all need to pick this up now."

That positive expectation communicates a message: We're a family, and we work together at whatever needs to be done. We always look out for the needs of people around us.

And saying such a thing calmly rather than yelling, "Get out here right now and help!" will do wonders for your psyche and everyone's day.

An Inside Job

The other day Hannah mentioned to me a talk that she and I had when she was a teenager.

"Remember when you told me how proud you were of the friends I was choosing? That meant so much to me, Dad. I think about that talk even now."

Back then I'd pointed out the positive characteristics of her friends and why I thought they were good companions. I also mentioned how pleased I was that Hannah was being so wise about the people she chose to spend her free time with.

How did this make her feel? It gave her a sense of accomplishment that captured and warmed her heart then and that she still remembers to this day.

What was I telling my daughter by sharing what I did? *I'm so proud of who you are, Hannah, and who you are becoming.*

What was Hannah hearing? *My dad is affirming my choices, which must mean I'm able to make wise choices.*

Now that's what I call an "inside job," focusing on the inside of the child—the character that matters most in the long run.

If you take time to know your child, focus on her unique qualities, and shower her with true encouragement—recognizing what she does and acknowledging her actual accomplishments—you will increase her confidence and life skills so that she'll continue to make wise choices in the future.

Good Question!

Are you raising a kid who has character or who *is* a character? What steps do you need to take to focus on the principle "It's who you are that counts"?

Five Tips for Raising a Great Kid

- Focus on cultivating your child's character rather than on making sure your child looks good to others.
- Don't miss your child's heart.
- Be specific in your thanks and encouragement.
- Take time to imprint your child with love and healthy self-worth.
- Celebrate your child's uniqueness.

SEVEN

THERE'S NO PLACE LIKE HOME

*Why everything important starts
and ends right in your living room.*

When our oldest kids were young, I used to drop them off at Grandma's to "pend" the night, as they called it then. They all loved going to Grandma's, but somehow that homing instinct pulled them back to their own nest. By the time I got home from dropping them off, I could count on the phone ringing. I didn't need caller ID in those days to know who it was.

Krissy.

It was always Krissy calling to talk about what they were doing and to chat with us. Of all our children, Krissy seemed to be most in tune with home, and her love of family continues today. She's what I call a "family-centered person," one whose homing instinct is strong. Although she loved going to Grandma's, there was a big part of her kid heart that simply missed Mom and Dad and wanted to include us in everything she did. She enjoyed Grandma, but there was nothing quite as good as home.

Home ought to be a refuge, a place your children return to again and again because it's where they feel most secure. The word *parent* comes from the Latin word *parentis*, which means "protector." And that means not only physical protection but also protection from conforming to the world's cookie-cutter view of who everybody else thinks your children should be. It's the place where children should be able to relax and be themselves. It's the place where they can learn, under your guiding hand and your unconditional love, how to respond to life's curveballs—those foisted at them as well as those they create themselves. It's the place where they learn what being responsible and caring for others mean.

Home ought to be a refuge, a place your children return to again and again because it's where they feel most secure.

It's the place where they realize that as part of the family, their contribution is important and necessary. It's the place where their hearts should reside.

But in order for all of those things to happen, you have to get off the activity wheel and make time for what really matters.

Are Your Hearts at Home?

When you choose to live an overcommitted life, keeping yourself and your kids running, day after day, like gerbils on a wheel, you're doing something else besides exhausting everyone. You're training your child to identify her heart with what is *outside* your home. That means dance lessons, play groups, soccer, French lessons, and all the other activities you schedule for your child will become her world and more important to her than a quiet evening at home eating popcorn and laughing at a movie with the family or discussing her day over dinner.

Is that really what you want for your family?

When you keep yourself and your kids on that activity wheel, the most profound lessons of life get squeezed out for lack of time. Instead of talking about what's really important, you spend most of your time talking with your spouse or a helping grandparent about who is going to pick up which kid where. Then dinners get squeezed out, and before long nobody is really talking to anybody anymore. You're too tired, so you turn on the television and continue living separate lives.

Your kids are watching you. Do they see you get more excited about catching the latest episode of *CSI* or talking with them about your values or your personal faith? Do you allow what isn't important over the long term to crowd out what is eternally important?

As your kids get older, you'll soon find that while they rarely listen to lectures—particularly moral lectures—they rarely miss life lessons, such as how Dad speaks when another driver cuts him off on the road or whether Mom encourages others or gossips when she talks on the phone.

If you invest time in your family and do things right, your kid, believe it or not, is going to want to please you. That's the secret your kids don't want you to know, but it's true. If your daughter has a strong family identity, then when somebody is passing marijuana around the car, saying, "Try it, you'll like it," she'll say, "I'm an Anderson, and we don't do that."

> **You can't give your child a more powerful antidote to negative peer pressure than to create a strong sense of family and values.**

If a group of boys is picking on somebody smaller, and one of your son's friends holds up the poor little guy and says, "Come on, Jason, it's your turn—hit him in the gut while I hold him," your son will say, "I'm an Alexander, and we don't treat people that way."

You can't give your child a more powerful antidote to negative peer pressure than to create a strong sense of family and values. But that happens only when you're spending time together as a family. It doesn't happen from pillar to post, as you run from activity to activity.

If you're a person of faith, it's crucial that you not only *say* you have faith but also practice that faith in ways children can see—every day. Because your child is watching you, how he or she responds to your beliefs gets down to the relationship *you* have with your Maker. If that relationship is real—not just something you wear on Sundays, or not mowing the grass on Sundays—and your children see that it's real, they'll be more likely to want to investigate that kind of faith themselves.

So integrate your faith into your day rather than waiting for the "big things" to talk to your Maker about. If you're overly busy and you try to shortcut the process by forcing your beliefs down your kids' throats or by dragging them to your place of worship anytime it's open, they will most likely rebel against your faith (and who could blame them?).

Here's an important consideration: When you check your bag at the Phoenix airport, the service representative puts a little tag on it that says "Transfer when it gets to Chicago," so that baggage handlers know to automatically transfer your bag to the next city, where your plane is landing. But there is no automatic transfer of faith from parent to child. Just because you hold to a certain faith and certain values doesn't mean your children will once they leave home. However, if you have a real relationship with your Maker and show it throughout the day, it will give your children pause to consider real faith in God.

There is no automatic transfer of faith from parent to child.

If you train your children *up,* not *down* (which means that you treat them the way *God* would have you train them, not the way *you* think they should be trained), they will probably either stay with your faith or return to your faith, even if they have a few (or many!) rocky moments along the way. But there is no Midas-muffler guarantee.

However, if you're around your kids enough, if you're a trusted and valued part of their lives, and if they can personally observe how relevant God is in your life, you give them the highest possibility for adopting your faith and values once they're out of your nest.

For, you see, home is where children learn heaps of lasting life lessons. Just take it from Opie Taylor.

A Trip Back to Mayberry . . .

Have you ever seen *The Andy Griffith Show*? I love that show. The TV series combined lovable characters and entertaining story lines with positive life lessons, and I could watch the reruns over and over. I've learned some of my most valuable life lessons from Mayberry sheriff Andy Taylor.

One of my favorite episodes is about nurturing and believing in your child, no matter what.[1] As the story begins, Opie is the proud owner of a new slingshot and is anxious to get outside to try it. Andy cautions his son to be careful with it, and Opie promises to shoot only at tin cans and such things.

He heads down the sidewalk, taking shots at bushes and tree trunks. Suddenly he spots movement in a tree and sends a stone flying, hitting a bird and knocking it to the ground.

Slowly Opie approaches the bird in stunned disbelief. As the bird lies motionless, the boy puts the slingshot in his back pocket, kneels down, and scoops the creature into his hands.

"Fly away," Opie cries. "*Please* fly away!" Gently he tosses the bird into the air to help it take off, but it falls lifeless to the grass.

Crying, Opie runs inside.

Later that afternoon, Andy returns home. When he picks up the newspaper from the sidewalk, he sees the dead bird and hears baby birds in a nearby tree. He peers up at the nest with a knowing look.

At supper that evening, as Opie picks at his food, Andy remarks to Aunt Bee that their neighbor ought to keep her cat inside because it had killed one of their songbirds.

That isn't possible, Aunt Bee replies. Mrs. Snyder has been gone for over a week and took her cat with her.

Opie leaves the table and rushes upstairs.

"Is he sick?" Aunt Bee wonders aloud.

Andy, however, knows better and follows Opie upstairs to his room. "You killed that bird, didn't you?" Andy asks.

Opie is silent at first, and then he nods.

Andy sternly reminds his son about his warning earlier in the day to be careful with the slingshot, and Opie says he is sorry.

"Being sorry is not the magic word that makes everything right again."

"That won't bring that bird back to life," Andy points out. "Being sorry is not the magic word that makes everything right again."

Then Andy makes a wise move. He walks across the room and opens the window. Outside on a nearby branch sits the nest with the motherless baby birds, whose hungry peeps fill the room.

"You hear that?" Andy says. "That's those young birds chirping for their momma that's never coming back. Now you just listen to that for a while."

What Andy has used with Opie is what I call "reality discipline." It's a term I coined in 1984. Basically it means to let nature take its course. For Opie, it was having to think about how shooting the mother bird affected those baby birds.

It allows for the reality of the situation to be the best teacher of the child.

If your son is supposed to write a science paper on one of the wonders of the universe and doesn't complete it, don't stay up until midnight doing it yourself. In fact, don't do anything about it at all. Just wait for reality to hit when he stands in front of his stern science teacher, who tells your son in no uncertain terms what she thinks of incomplete projects.

If your little girl goes into her older sister's room and gets into her makeup, don't intervene in the situation and help her clean it up before her sister gets home. Unless she thinks to clean it up herself, don't bother. Just wait to see what her older sister is going to say, and let the two of them work it out.

Every decision we make has consequences. If you let those natural results teach your child rather than using arbitrary reward and punishment or "rescuing" your child, you'll be preparing him or her to live responsibly.

A Little Reality Is All It Takes

Reality discipline helps kids develop internal guidance systems rather than parents controlling their kids' actions. As a parent, my job is not to control my child. Not even God controls us. He doesn't reach down, push us against a wall, and say, "You *will* acknowledge Me."

Not that some parents don't try. Sande and I knew a guy whose kids sat on our couch like birds on a fence—legs crossed and hands folded as they waited for their father to give them permission to move! But he wasn't doing his kids any favors by making them into puppets yanked around by rules.

Kids who are easily controlled are pushovers with their peer group. I want my child to learn to say *no* when told to "drink this, shoot this, snort this." And that kind of training isn't accomplished by "You'd better do this or else," one-way discussions.

Kids who are easily controlled are pushovers with their peer group.

Discipline may be something I do "to" my daughter, but it's also something I nurture in her so that she'll learn to make wise decisions herself. Inner discipline is infinitely more important than outer conformity, especially when your child turns eighteen and leaves home. When you're no longer around to set the rules, what kind of character and self-discipline will your child exercise?

That's why it wouldn't be a good idea to tell Opie, "Here's your new slingshot. Now, if you shoot the birds or the neighbors' windows, I'm going to take it away and ground you for a week!" Sure, you need to assess the boy's maturity to handle the slingshot and remind him to be careful. But if you threaten him with punishment before he's even pulled back the sling, you've said to him, "This slingshot is probably more than you can handle, so when [not *if*] you mess up, here's what you'll have coming to you."

That isn't reality discipline. It's the kind of traditional discipline that hasn't worked for years. It uses fear of punishment to get a child to conform on the outside. Reality discipline works through natural consequences, mutual respect, and a belief in the best that is in your child.

The Truth About Consequences

By letting Opie experience the consequences of his actions, Andy helped the boy understand the relationship between his decisions and their effects on him and those around him. If Andy had given him "a whippin'" and called it a day, Opie might have gotten the message that he should listen to his dad more carefully next time. But as a child grows, punishment loses its sting. The day comes when Dad and Mom aren't there to administer the consequences. What then?

The nice thing about childhood is that consequences are rather tame compared to those later in life. Cheating on the seventh-grade math test has fewer consequences than cheating on income taxes. By allowing Opie to suffer consequences when the stakes were lower, Andy nurtured in his son an inner responsibility that would help prevent more painful consequences down the road.

So when should you use consequences in raising kids? Believe it or not, the teachable moment doesn't have to happen immediately after your child doesn't do what he or she is supposed to, or tells a lie, or comes home late.

Let's say your thirteen-year-old daughter smart-mouths you. Two hours later she wants to be driven to the mall to meet her friends. You might reply, "I don't feel like driving you to the mall today."

"*Mom,*" your child might say, "I want to go to the mall!"

"Honey," you could reply, "you're not hearing what I'm saying. I don't feel like doing it today."

That kid will not give up, and pretty soon you'll have an opportunity to tell her straight out what is on your mind.

"Well, to be specific, I'm still not happy about the way you talked to me around nine thirty this morning when I asked you to take the garbage out and check on your baby brother. I didn't like your attitude, I didn't like the look on your face, and I certainly didn't appreciate the words you uttered under your breath—which I did hear, by the way."

For the two of you to reconcile, that daughter has to acknowledge her wrongdoing. Otherwise, the natural consequence is a rift in your relationship.

Do You React . . . or Respond?

When your kids have done something wrong, do you shoot yourself in the foot? Do you *react* rather than *respond*? Reacting means that you let your emotions get the better of you. Children are master manipulators, and they can tick us off like no one else can. Responding means that you think first, and *then* speak or act.

Look at it this way. If the doctor says, "You responded to your medication," that's good. If the doctor says, "You reacted to your medication," that's bad.

Let's say you're driving, and your son says, "Mommy, I want to be a snowboarder when I grow up."

"What?" you say. "That's the stupidest thing I've ever heard. There's no way you could be a snowboarder. We live in Florida, and we don't even get snow in the winter. Are you out of your mind?"

That's reacting. Answering without thinking in the situation.

This is responding: "Oh, a snowboarder." (Pause to show you're dreaming and thinking about it too.) "Can you imagine what it would be like? To be out there with all that snow, just flying through the air like a bird? It sure would be exciting, wouldn't it? In the mornings, you could suit up, and you could spend the whole day in the snow."

Sure, you live in Florida and just watching Shaun White during the last Olympics gave you the willies. But why shoot your child's dream out of the water? He will eventually realize that being a snowboarder probably won't happen. You don't need to hurry the realization along.

There's a way to stick to your guns without shooting yourself, or your children, in the foot. Instead of reacting, respond by saying, "Tell me more about that."

B Doesn't Happen Until A Is Completed

Another great way to teach reality discipline is through the principle of "B doesn't happen until A is completed." You never have to change this strategy. It works every time with every age. If you've asked your child to do something, and it's not done, you don't move on to the next event—no matter what the event is.

Let's say your ten-year-old daughter is supposed to practice her flute and put the dishes in the dishwasher. Clearly, neither are done. Two hours later your daughter is supposed to go to her best friend's house to play. She gets her favorite toys packed and in the car, and then she says, "C'mon, Mom, let's go."

Your response? "We're not going." Then turn your back and walk away.

If your child follows you, don't announce your strategy. It works better if the child has to figure it out for herself.

Within a few minutes, your daughter is panicking. "But, Mom, we're supposed to be at Cyndi's in ten minutes!"

Your response? "We're not going."

As your daughter pursues you and sees your determination, she'll be ready to hear the reason. "I asked you to practice your flute and put the dishes in the dishwasher. Until those are done, we're not going anywhere."

I can guarantee you that your daughter will move double time to get those two tasks done—especially because she'll receive two phone calls from her friend in the meantime, wondering where she is.

Stick to your guns. Don't feel sorry for the kid and back off—"Well, I'll do it this one time."

Most of all, parent, stick to your guns. Don't feel sorry for the kid and back off—"Well, I'll do it this one time . . ."

If you do it this time, you'll find yourself doing it again and again and again.

Here's a caveat: When you start applying these techniques, a child's attitudes and behaviors will often get worse for a time. That means you're on the right track.

The most important thing is to be consistent in your actions. Keep the ball of responsibility in your child's court, not yours. Don't harass, threaten, or warn your kid. Don't say, "Well, if you had gotten your jobs done . . ." Instead, simply state that the jobs aren't done, and until they are, the next event won't happen. A child of any age can understand that reasoning.

It comes down to this: Seeing the changes you want implemented is more about *you* than it is about your child. If you mean what you say and say what you mean, your child will get it.

Smart Parents . . .

- Love their kids unconditionally.
- Offer encouragement.
- Say no.
- Don't nag.
- Stick to their guns . . . without shooting themselves in the foot.

After the Consequences

Let's return to Opie's story to look at what should happen *after* using consequences.

Once Andy has let Opie sit with the results of his actions, he doesn't prolong the lesson the following day out of anger. He allows a new day to bring a new start. Rather than laying into the boy all over again for his mistake, Andy warmly wishes him, "Mornin', son."

Opie is sitting on the porch steps with a box cradled in his lap. Curious, Andy asks what the boy is doing. Opie replies that he's fixing breakfast for the baby birds he has adopted and named Winkin', Blinkin', and Nod. When Aunt Bee comes out onto the porch a few minutes later, Andy tells her that Opie is owning up to the consequences of his actions by mothering the baby birds.

You see, not only does Andy follow his reality discipline with a fresh start for Opie; he also affirms the change in his son, who took responsibility to care for the hatchlings.

"If you care for those baby birds well," Andy tells Opie after the boy has fed them for a few days, "you'll be proud of them when they're grown."

That's a message for you, too, Mom and Dad. When you focus on raising your kids as well as you can—nurturing them by giving them responsibility, holding them accountable for their actions, and showing them grace when they fail—then in all probability they'll grow to be mature and responsible, the kind of adults you hope they'll become.

Most parents tend to direct praise at their children's behavior: "My, you're a good boy because you played so nicely with your friends this afternoon." The child assumes he's held in high esteem because he did well. But it's much more important to acknowledge kids for *who they are* than for *what they've done*. Performance isn't the important thing. But the attitude they have while trying to accomplish a task is.

An encouraging statement might be, "Now you're getting it!" or "Hey, it looks like that extra practice is really paying off!"

When I'm asked to describe my kids, you'll hear me say such things as, "They sincerely care about other people." Or "I'm so proud of who my daughter *is*—the way she has a heart for and gives to others." I try to notice those traits and encourage them as best I can, to let her know Dad is watching.

When Opie releases Winkin', Blinkin', and Nod at the end of the episode, he breathes a sigh of relief that the birds all flew off okay. Andy affirms the efforts of his son, who looks down at the cage with a touch of loss.

"The cage looks so empty," Opie says.

Andy agrees, but then he wisely adds a final note of encouragement. "But don't the trees seem nice and full?" he says as birdsong fills the air.

There truly is no place like home. It's the place where everything important begins and ends—right in your living space. It should be a place of grace, of second chances. It's also a place where the right attitudes are encouraged through the right kind of praise.

Do You Believe . . . in Your Child?

Will you indulge me by letting me mention another favorite episode of mine from *The Andy Griffith Show*? I honestly think this series should be part of every child's elementary education—and probably part of every parent's education in raising children.

In this episode, Opie tells Andy and Deputy Barney Fife that he met a man named Mr. McBeevee who "walks around up in the treetops."[2] Mr. McBeevee wears a "great, big, shiny silver hat," says Opie, and "he sort of jingles" when he walks, "just like he had rings on his fingers and bells on his toes." That comes "from all the things hanging on his belt." To top it off, Opie tells his dad and Barney that Mr. McBeevee can "make smoke come out of his ears."

"He even gave me a quarter," Opie adds, pulling the coin from his shirt pocket.

Andy, who has been listening to his son with amusement, asks if what he just heard is correct: that Mr. McBeevee, the fellow Opie just described in the most outlandish terms, gave him the quarter.

Sure, Opie tells his father, as naturally as if men in trees handed out quarters every day. Mr. McBeevee said Opie had earned it.

Andy, who is now bewildered, asks where Opie *really* got the quarter.

Opie stands by his answer: Mr. McBeevee. If his dad would like to hear it from Mr. McBeevee himself, they should go to the woods together and ask *him* to tell his father the story.

Andy, who is now uncomfortable with Opie's tall tale and wants to get to the bottom of it, takes him up on the idea, and the two of them set off.

Once they reach the woods, Opie calls up into the trees for Mr. McBeevee, begging him to come down and tell his father about the quarter.

As you might expect, there's no reply.

The two wander through the forest as Opie calls again and again up into the trees for Mr. McBeevee. But still there is no response.

Finally Andy tells Opie it's time to head home.

Back in Opie's bedroom, Andy confronts his son regarding the difference between make-believe stories and the truth. He reminds Opie of the fun the two of them were having that morning talking about Opie's make-believe horse, "Blackie," and points out that Blackie was simply made up from the boy's imagination.

Perhaps the same is true for Mr. McBeevee, Andy suggests. Perhaps Opie also made up Mr. McBeevee for fun. Andy is quick to note that there's nothing wrong with that, as long as what his son imagines doesn't get in the way of his responsibilities and cause him to avoid what really happened. He then tells Opie that at times the responsible thing to do is to own up to reality rather than hiding behind what he imagines to be true.

All Opie has to do, says Andy, is admit that Mr. McBeevee is make-believe, and the whole incident will be forgotten. But if he doesn't, Andy adds, he thinks Opie knows what's coming.

Opie begins to deny Mr. McBeevee but then stops. "I can't, Pa. Mr. McBeevee isn't make-believe. He's real."

"*Opie* . . ." begins Andy.

"Don't you believe me, Pa?" Opie pleads. "Don't you, Pa?"

Andy considers his son for a moment and then sighs. He nods. "I believe you," he says. He pats Opie on the leg, leaves his room, and walks downstairs to where Barney and Aunt Bee are waiting.

At first, Barney is relieved that Opie didn't receive a spanking, but when he hears that Andy told Opie that he believed him, the deputy is beside himself. What Opie is saying is *impossible*, Barney declares.

Andy points out that many times he tells Opie to believe things that must seem impossible to his son. He certainly has a point. It must be difficult for a young child to accept that strangers offering candy are up to no good, and that discipline is for the child's best.

Do you believe in your child despite all evidence to the contrary?

But, Barney protests, what about all that talk about Mr. McBeevee's silver hat and how he jingles when he walks? Andy isn't sure what to make of it all, but he says that at times you have to decide whether to take a step of faith to believe in someone.

"But you do believe in Mr. McBeevee?" asks Barney.

"No . . . no," Andy says thoughtfully. "I do believe in Opie."

Though Opie's story seems completely fantastical, Sheriff Taylor takes an admirable step. He believes in his son in spite of all the evidence to the contrary.

Do you believe in your child despite all evidence to the contrary?

I can't underscore enough the importance of believing in your child, come flunking grades or your child being on a first-name basis in the principal's office. Believing in your child is one of the best investments you can make. I ought to know, since my mother was the queen of belief in little Kevin, who was always in trouble. Without her influence, or the influence of a special teacher who believed in me—despite all evidence to the contrary—I wouldn't be in the trenches of helping kids and families today.

Your belief in your child, your confidence in who he is, will inspire him to move toward your vision of what he can be. When you communicate by your words and actions, "I believe in you and expect the best of you," your child will strive to honor that.

When Opie Lets You Down

At the end of the episode, Andy heads back into the woods to mull over Opie's insistence that Mr. McBeevee is real. Shaking his head, he says Mr. McBeevee's name aloud in disbelief—and is astonished to hear someone answer from above! Seconds later, a man in spiked boots climbs down one of the trees. He's a telephone lineman, and when he reaches the ground, he introduces himself as Mr. McBeevee.

Andy stands there in wonder. "You walk around in the trees. Silver hat. You jingle," he says, looking at Mr. McBeevee's tool belt. "You can make smoke come out of your ears, can't you? Mr. McBeevee, I can't tell you how glad I am to meet you!" Andy shakes the man's hand vigorously. "I'm Andy Taylor, Opie's dad!"

Well, you may think, *Andy's belief in his child paid off* that *time.*

But even if Opie *had* been lying, that belief still would have paid off. It would have appealed to the boy's desire to live up to his father's expectations—and triggered disappointment in letting his dad down.

Let's assume for a moment that you take Sheriff Taylor's approach—and it turns out that your child is making the whole thing up. Mr. McBeevee is a complete fabrication, and your little rascal knows it. What should you do?

When your kid tells you what you know for a fact is a whopper, you might say, "So, your friend Steven saw Mr. McBeevee too? I think I'll call Steven's mother right now and ask her about that." Get down to where the rubber meets the road. There's a consequence for your child's lying: your broken trust and the guilt he feels for having disappointed you—as well as his embarrassment at having his lie exposed.

Here's something else you might do. Next time your son asks to go someplace he goes every day after school, tell him *no.*

"No?" he'll ask, surprised. "Why no? You always let me go there."

"There's no reason for me to believe you'll *be* there," you could reply.

"What do you mean? I *always* go there."

"Well, do you remember what you said about Mr. McBeevee? If I couldn't trust you then, why should I trust you now? You're going to have to build up your credibility again. So the answer today is *no.*"

That's how I'd handle it so that he sees there's a consequence for lying. Again, it's the principle of reality discipline. But once your child's failure is in the open, don't carry on. Nobody likes a bone digger. Do you like to be reminded of your failures? Well, neither does your child. Remember your child's need for grace and encouragement.

Many people won't believe in your child. If there's one person left standing in the world who does, that person should be you.

And that, as well as the fact that there's no place like home, is what I learned in Mayberry.

Good Question!

How will being aware that your child is watching you change your words and actions this week?

The Six Most Important Lessons from Home

- You don't need to be the "heavy." Let reality be your child's teacher.
- Learn to respond rather than react.
- B doesn't happen until A is completed.
- Discipline is more than something you do. It's something you nurture inside your kids so they learn to make their own wise decisions.
- Live out your beliefs and faith. Your children are watching.
- Believe in your child. That confidence will go a long way in inspiring your child to fly in achieving his or her potential.

EIGHT

THE POWER OF POSITIVE EXPECTATIONS

Why you hold all the aces at home and at school.

Parent, I'll tell you a secret. You hold all the aces. Your kid probably wouldn't even have fresh underwear without you.

But take a look around at the supermarket, at the mall, and even in your own kitchen. What do you see? I see two-and-a-half-foot-tall kids making all sorts of demands on adults.

"No, I don't want Rice Krispies. I want Cocoa Puffs!"

And the demands only grow with the height of the children.

"Where's the car keys? I want the car keys . . . now!"

We're surrounded by a lot of self-centered, hedonistic kids with a one-way agenda: *It's all about me.*

Why is it these days that so many children act disrespectfully? And why do we parents get caught in the roles of threatening and cajoling, yet never get anywhere?

Well, kids do what they do simply because they've gotten away with it!

It all comes down to who is really in charge of your family. Is it you or your child? Are you concerned about being your child's friend, about not wounding her "psyche," about making sure your son is happy and successful? If so, you're most likely snowplowing your child's road in life, smoothing all the bumps so that your child never has to be uncomfortable or go out of his or her way.

And what does that make you? The hired help, not the parent.

As a result, today's kids are growing more powerful. They're all about "me, me, me" and "gimme." They are held accountable less and have fewer responsibilities in the family. To them, family is about not what they can give but what they can get. They rarely consider others before themselves because they've never been taught to think that way.

Kids do what they do simply because they've gotten away with it!

Every child plays a daily trial-and-error game designed to get the best of you. And he's motivated to win, because then dear old Mom or Dad will do anything he says. That means if he tries something, and it works, he'll try it again. But he'll ramp up his efforts a little. Instead of simply crying when he doesn't get his treat, he'll add a little kicking, too. If slamming the door causes you to go trotting after your teenage daughter to hand over the car keys as she wanted, she'll be more dramatic the next time she wants them. Children are masters at manipulation. Don't think your child isn't manipulating you.

Your child is constantly watching to see who's in charge. How you respond to being in charge has a lot to do with your own background, your own dreams for your child, and what kinds of expectations you heap on that child.

Great Expectations Gone Awry

Agustin began parenting his newborn son, fresh from the hospital, as if the boy were cramming for a final.[1] The schedule included incessant reading, music by Mozart and Beethoven, and hours together watching educational TV programs. The man had great hopes for his son.

Agustin had written a short story about a gifted child who grew up to become a scientist and world leader in an intergalactic movement to help humankind. He'd also developed a "Magic Formula," a "secret technique designed to accelerate the energy in fertile women so as to produce gifted children," and he gave this formula to his live-in partner, Cathy.

At just six and a half weeks of age, Adragon (named in honor of the Chinese Year of the Dragon) allegedly spoke his first word: *hello*. At age three the boy was studying science. At age five, his IQ was four hundred—at least according to Agustin's testing—which would have made him perhaps "the greatest intellect in history."

Adragon was only eight when he entered Cabrillo College, where he reportedly learned calculus by age nine—three years ahead of Einstein. At age ten he transferred to the University of California, Santa Cruz, to pursue computational mathematics, enrolling for double the normal student load. He graduated a year later, at eleven years of age, the youngest college graduate ever, according to *The Guinness Book of World Records*.

In interviews, Agustin called Adragon his "greatest creation" and "probably the most unique child that any generation has seen since the time of Da Vinci."

Agustin saw Adragon's time with friends, however, as wasted—a point on which he and Cathy disagreed. After school he would "whisk the poor kid away and rush him home to cram more facts in his head," said Lewis Keizer, director of the Popper-Keizer School for gifted children, where Adragon was enrolled for a short time.

On September 19, 1988, law-enforcement officers stormed Agustin's house with a "warrant based on an affidavit signed by AD's mother: Agustin's 'Grand Plan' for AD amounted to child abuse; AD was in danger; Agustin possessed a cache of weapons; AD would be better served living with [his mother]." Officers snatched Adragon from the house, away from Agustin and his "Grand Plan."

Today, achievement is no longer the most important thing in Adragon's life. Friends are, he says. Known by those friends simply as "James," the former prodigy still loves his father deeply.

Learning how to be a kid, though, has been a major adjustment. That, admits James, "might be harder than calculus."

Was Agustin wrong to have dreams for his child? Doesn't everyone, child and adult, dream of something?

I still remember as a Little Leaguer walking up to home plate, hoping to plaster the ball out of the park, and hearing my father yell his dream from the stands: "Hit a home run!"

Those words echoing in my mind made me much more desperate to connect with the ball.

In every family, there is a clash of two very common dreams—a child's dream of pleasing his parents, and a parent's dream that her kids will experience the life she wants them to.

Sweet Dreams?

Your own childhood experiences and adult hopes will always tend to color how you encourage—or discourage—your kids as they grow. If athletics was your ticket to popularity in school, you may find yourself pushing your child into sports when he is content with chess club. Or you may remember the sting of failing to make it into law school, so you drive your child to make it through that door.

Many of your dreams are healthy. You want your children to receive a good education, to grow in love, and to be accepted by others. But when your dreams clash with their personalities, or you hone their abilities to the neglect of their healthy development in other areas, or you cause your child to be the gerbil constantly running on the wheel, getting nowhere she wants to be, you're stepping out of line.

And here's the secret: Because your kids want your affirmation more than anything else, they'll be likely to go along with your

"Grand Plan," even if they're not the least bit interested in it. Why else do you see so many children with miserable faces at piano recitals? They're dressed up and no place they want to be. But there's proud Momma in the crowd, videotaping the entire venture with a smile.

Because your kids want your affirmation more than anything else, they'll be likely to go along with your "Grand Plan," even if they're not the least bit interested in it.

Then there's another mother I talked to recently. Her nine-year-old daughter had a singing role in a Christmas play. The girl practiced and practiced, but when she got up to perform, she bungled the words badly. Though she carried on courageously, she began crying as soon as she was offstage.

The mother encouraged her daughter but told me in private, "I was actually pleased to see this happen. Because of her personality, she needs to learn how to deal with failure a little bit better. I was just thankful that I could be there so we could talk about it."

That mom has her priorities straight. She values building character over a performance no one would remember three weeks later. She also made sure she was there to witness her daughter's performance, which gave her the chance to offer immediate, helpful input.

What's Your Dream?

What do you want your child to be doing at age eighteen? More to the point, *who* do you want your child to be? Do you envision a charismatic 4.0 scholar with Ivy League schools clamoring for his admission? How about at age twenty-two? A professional athlete? A highly paid attorney straight out of law school?

Many parents won't admit such things, but their actions make it obvious what they're aiming for. To reach these dreams for their children, some parents will do anything—including their kids' homework. Roughly one-fourth of parents admit to occasionally doing their child's homework when their child is too tired or the work is too hard.[2]

As a counselor, I find that many parental expectations are born of good intentions. One man might buck his family history, working his way through high school and college to become a successful businessman. Not wanting his children to be subjected to the kind of life he escaped, he pushes them to achieve—until he pushes them right out of his life.

Or a mother, feeling she married "beneath" herself, wants to spare her daughter that fate. The woman harps on the girl's posture, dress, exercise, and general hygiene—missing the point that a good marriage depends almost entirely on character and has almost nothing to do with appearance.

But parents who take stock of their own experiences can avoid repeating hurtful patterns with their children. Take a moment to reflect on your own childhood and the corresponding expectations you have for your kids.

One of the most irritating things for children is forever being

Take a Look Back

Honestly ask yourself the following questions:
- What was my childhood like? What did my parents expect of me?
- How have my childhood disappointments and losses influenced the expectations I have for my children today?
- How does my desire to look like a good and competent parent put even more pressure on my kids?
- In what specific way(s) am I pushing each of my children?

compared to siblings and friends. And unless you have only one child, all parents are guilty of this from time to time.

"Do you remember when Jimmy first did that?" you might ask your spouse when your little daughter shows you her somersault.

Without meaning to, you've just told your child, "Your older brother did that three years earlier than you did. What's the big deal?"

Comparisons are always misleading because no two kids will ever be exactly alike. This is a big world; we need analytical people, funny people, managers, athletes, followers, leaders, you name it. What does it matter if second-born Samuel isn't as quick with numbers as firstborn Alan? If Sammy becomes a talk-show host, he can *hire* people like Alan to keep his books. Why not instead realize that to make the world go round, it takes all kinds—and accept and nurture your children's gifts as they develop?

Your dreams should be in line with God's design and gifting for your girl or boy. Educator and radio teacher Chuck Swindoll told me that you could translate Proverbs 22:6, "Train a child in the way he should go," as "train a child *according to his bent.*"

So why not allow your child to go according to his or her bent rather than trying to follow yours? You both have everything to gain.

Blowouts and Slow Leaks

Most kids aren't all that adept at articulating their emotions. They won't come up to you and say, "Can we talk? I'm feeling that I can never measure up to what you want me to be. So that's why I'm arguing over petty things, disrupting family activities, and picking on my little sister."

A kid's not going to say that, but if that's how he feels, you'll probably see it in his behavior. He may start getting mouthy with one or both parents. If an outsider were to watch him for a few days, he might say, "You have an angry kid."

My advice: Don't ignore the emotional duress. Dr. James Dobson calls this the "Blowout vs. the Slow Leak Syndrome." If you've built up tension over the years between you and your child because of your expectations, don't let it leak into his adult years. Address the tension now—but do it sensitively. You don't want the Slow Leak Syndrome to become a "blowup."[3]

If you've built up tension over the years between you and your child because of your expectations, don't let it leak into his adult years.

No radical changes can be made overnight.

But you can start with an apology.

"Honey, I'm sorry," you might tell your daughter. "Moms and dads make mistakes too. I've been too hard on you, and I'm sorry. I want you to know how proud I am of you, even when I don't act like it sometimes."

Thank Goodness They're Normal!

When a child is in the womb, we pray for nine months that he'll emerge looking normal. Then, even if he does, we never accept normal again! We want him to forever rise above the average.

For every "success" story—say, an inner city boy who made it out of the ghetto and bought a new home for his mom—I could tell you a dozen about a suburbanite who bent her entire family around a daughter's potential gymnastics career, only to discover that her little girl didn't have what it took to compete on a national level. Or a mom who woke up all her kids early Saturday mornings to take the oldest boy to his swim meets in another town—and then became bitter when Junior decided he wanted to race motorcycles instead.

There's something wonderful about having a normal, average kid who doesn't feel pressured to be the top student in class or a starting quarterback. In my high-school class, there were some kids we all thought would make it big in the "real world," but they didn't go much further than the school parking lot. If your child is average, celebrate. I'm so glad I have normal kids, kids who enjoy life, feel good about themselves, and give generously to other people.

Those inner qualities are worth much more to me than any string of As, or seeing my child's face flash across ESPN.

Seven Ways to Use Positive Expectations

As you've reflected on your own childhood, the expectations your parents had for you, and the resulting expectations you have for your kids now, you might have had a eureka moment. "Wow, I really have been pressuring my kids too much."

But you don't want your kids to get away with no expectations either. So how can you turn your expectations into positive ones, not only for your benefit, but also for your child's best interests? Following are seven ways to make this transition.

1. Give 'Em Grace

When a sheep is a little out of line, what does a good shepherd do? He doesn't whack the sheep over the head until it submits. He gives the sheep a little tap with his rod to get it back in line.

But that works only when there is a relationship between the shepherd and the sheep. Otherwise, that little sheep couldn't care less what the shepherd is doing.

In your home, you're the shepherd and your children are your sheep. Many view a shepherd's rod and staff as instruments of punishment and pain, but David, the psalmist, said that the rod and staff "comfort" (Psalm 23:4). The rod, in fact, was used for rescuing and protecting, not to wallop the animals black and blue. When you think of discipline that way, it can change the way you respond to your children.

Positive expectation is full of grace; it allows for failure. When little Darcy whines for a candy bar in the grocery store, expecting the best allows you not to panic. You say, "Silly you! Don't you re-

Assume the best and act on that.

member we just discussed that?" and then move on. Don't make it a bigger deal than it is. Maybe she really did forget your chat outside the supermar-

ket. Your challenge is to assume the best and act on that.

"Nice try," the gracious parent might say when a child misses the mark. "There's always next time." Every child will get off center occasionally. When needed, just give him a little tap to get him back on track. The important thing isn't that he's walking exactly in the center of the path, like a robot would, but that he's going in the right direction.

After all, do *you* always make the right choices? Do you always respond to others in the right tone of voice or behave your best?

I sure don't. None of us do. Positive expectations give Junior or Juniorette a little space to be human.

2. Build Boundaries

Positive expectations serve as guardrails on that wide path your child must travel. Let's go back to the grocery-store example. Using positive expectations, you've made it clear when your kids can and can't have candy. It's normal—not rebellion—when they test you on this, asking to buy a Super Sugar Sucker to eat on the way home before dinner. Just smile and say, "Nice try, honey. You *know* I'm not going to let you have that, don't you?"

Little Missy smiles, maybe laughs, and puts down the sucker. Yes, she does know the boundaries. There are times she can have candy and times she can't. She understands the boundaries, and she appreciates the fact that you talk to her as if she does: "You *know* I'm not going to let you have that, don't you?"

You can even laugh with her: "Are you being silly? Maybe we should buy lots of potato chips, too, and chocolate milk and ice cream, and eat them in the car; then we'll be *really* hungry for dinner, won't we?"

A mom with negative expectations might meet the request for that Super Sugar Sucker, fearing she's about to face another public scene. Or she might refuse, even though everything about her demeanor is screaming panic: "Put that down! Don't ask me again! What were you thinking? What's the matter with you? Didn't I already tell you no in the car? Have you lost your hearing?"

The child recognizes that Mom is getting pretty uptight about a simple request, and all of a sudden it dawns on her: *Hey, if I'm not mistaken, I've found a chink in Mom's armor. Let's see how far I can take this thing.*

Positive expectations can even build boundaries with teenagers. Here's how:

"Dad," my son, Kevin II, said as he headed out one evening, "I'll be down at Peter Piper Pizza with some friends."

"Sure," I said, "have fun. Just get back at a reasonable hour."

"A reasonable hour?" he asked. "When's a reasonable hour?"

That's a question I've never answered straight out with any of my children. "Oh, you know," I might reply, "a reasonable hour."

Dr. Leman, you might think, *are you nuts? You don't get much more of an open door than that!* It's true that many parents would be thrilled if their teens asked what time they needed to return at night—and you can bet they'd tell them! But if you're after long-term training in character, you have to realize that you won't always be there to make sure your child gets home by 11:00 p.m. What about when he's on his own? What will he do then?

So when is a *reasonable hour?* Obviously it isn't four in the morning. Here in Tucson, we have public curfews. If Kevin II returned then, privileges with the car would end quickly.

Instead of just telling him a specific time, I wanted *him* to think through and decide when a realistic, reasonable hour was.

If you're always drawing lines in the sand, then your children never have the opportunity to draw their own lines.

If I were to tell my son that he needed to be home at 11:00 p.m., the final line would be drawn. He might *want* to stay out later, but what would keep him from doing so?

If you're always drawing lines in the sand, then your children never have the opportunity to draw their own lines. And learning to draw their own lines helps kids embrace what's good and loving—and keeps them from doing what hurts them and others.

The goal is to let kids learn inner responsibility that will carry them through no matter where they are. The trick is giving them enough age-appropriate freedom to make their own decisions. Expecting the best of your children keeps the tennis ball of life in their court.

You'd be amazed how following that principle will take the heat out of the words in your house.

3. Play on Your Child's Team

When our daughter Lauren was eleven, she declared that one of her biggest treats was having friends over. After all, with some distance in years between her and her next older sister, Hannah, she was often at home with just Dad and Mom. So I tried to be mindful of that question forever dancing in her brain: *Can I have someone over?* I do as much as I can to give her what she honestly needs. In other words, I play on her team.

Families with negative expectations become hostile rivals, each side warily circling the other, looking for a weakness to exploit. You can't have an intimate relationship if you're constantly circling each other in the family ring, looking for a takedown hold. It's much healthier—and happier—to be on each other's team.

Are you on your child's team? Would your child say you are?

Being on your children's team doesn't mean dropping everything you have to do to please them. It means simply trying to help meet their real, honest-to-goodness needs whenever you can. If your kids see you going out of your way to meet legitimate needs, they won't be so quick to throw tantrums when you must occasionally say no. But when you find yourself saying no to almost everything they ask, take a swift look at why. Is it because you're all running like gerbils on a wheel—going and going like the Energizer Bunny, but not getting anywhere that matters?

4. Learn from Failure

I recently received a letter from my high school stating that I'd been elected to its "Wall of Fame." That was one of the funniest things I'd ever heard, because my only claim to fame in high school was my unbroken record of poor grades.

I graduated fourth from the bottom in my class. My high-school counselor even told me he couldn't get me into reform school. I applied to 160 colleges and universities, and none of them wanted me. Not only was I a terrible student; I was a discipline problem.

But I couldn't wait to tell my mother about this postgraduation honor. After all, she was the one who went to school and talked to the teachers when I repeatedly skipped classes.

My high-school counselor even told me he couldn't get me into reform school.

"Ma," I said, after I had read her the letter, "I guess we came out on top of that one, didn't we? We sure got the last laugh." And we did. My mother, who was ninety-two at the time (talk about waiting a long time for some parental reward!), nearly laughed her dentures out as we talked about my accepting the award.

Failure isn't everything. It's not even the only thing. It's simply an indicator that a child needs more time to develop. If your child is going to fail—and roughly 100 percent do—do you want him or her to learn to fail gracefully in the safety of your home and under your loving direction? Kids need a safe place to mispronounce words, say ridiculously stupid things (one girl I know wondered how they made ice cubes in Australia, since it was so hot), or try a clothes combination that only a clown would love. So don't treat failure as a shameful roadblock; treat it as a stepping-stone.

Kids often say, "I can't do that. It's too hard." Many are simply more afraid of the stigma of failure than they are of testing their abilities. When your kids say things like that, gently pull them aside and say, "Hey, go ahead and give it your best shot. If it doesn't work, no big deal. At least you've learned that lesson." It helps kids if you keep failure in a healthy context: It's a normal, natural part of life. You might tell them about one of your own failures to show that it wasn't the end of the world for you.

> **Kids often say, "I can't do that. It's too hard." Many are simply more afraid of the stigma of failure than they are of testing their abilities.**

Minor-league baseball games are exciting to watch precisely because minor leaguers get ample opportunities to make mistakes. In fact, baseball players who are brought up too soon from the minor leagues rarely do well in the majors. Managers like to "season" them. That's why the idea of allowing your kids to fail at home is such a positive one. You want your child's mettle to be tested in the "minor leagues," where she can feel comfortable finding the courage to risk and will have your encouragement to keep trying when she fails.

5. *Choose Your Words Carefully*

Actress Gwyneth Paltrow has described herself as "the daddy's girl of all time."[4] Her father, Bruce Paltrow, took Gwyneth to Paris when she was ten so that "she could see the city for the first time with a man who would always love her." Gwyneth remembers the way her father's words provided "a huge safety net" for her.

"My father had that incredible Jewish warmth," said Gwyneth, whose dad died a few days after her thirtieth birthday. She remembers him "really bolstering us [Paltrow and her brother] all the time. And when you're 9 years old and you're hearing that you are the best person, it gets in there, and you think, 'OK, I'm not going to be afraid to try things, because I'm always loved no matter what.' "[5]

A wise proverb says, "The tongue has the power of life and death" (Proverbs 18:21). I see this truth played out in families across the country.

Everyone knows the saying "sticks and stones may break my bones, but words will never hurt me." The truth is, words do have the power to tear down; some words, once said, are hard to take back.

But words also have a miracle-working power: "The tongue of the wise brings healing," says another wise proverb (Proverbs 12:18). Paltrow said that her father "was the one person in your life that you always think, 'I'm safe because they're there, and they're so smart, and they know everything, and I can always go to them.' "[6]

Isn't this how you want your kids to think of you? The right words help your child see you as a safe place, someone who's always approachable and there for them.

"That kills me, when I think about it," Paltrow added. "It totally breaks my heart, how lucky I am."[7] Paltrow is indeed lucky. Don't you want to give your own children the same kind of affirmation?

6. Have the Conversation

No, I'm not talking about *that* conversation. Not the birds and bees. What I have in mind may be even more important.

At some point you need to say to your son or daughter something like this: "No matter what you do in life, I'll always love you. You may be mean to your sister, you may not be nice to us, you may reject our faith or become a liar, a thief, or some combination of all of the above—but I will *always* love you. That will *never* change."

What's the point of telling your child that? you might ask. *Wouldn't it be better to just strike a little fear in your child's heart by telling him or her to stay in line, or else?*

Many kids rebel because they feel that all their parents care about is having kids who turn out according to their expectations. "All my parents want is to boast about the things I do in front of their peers," Jonathan told me. "So every week I have to accomplish something big or new to make them feel good about themselves. I'm sick of all of it."

Marisa saw it from a different perspective. "Every time we go anywhere, my dad says, 'Hey, just warning you, you better behave.' I think that after about thirteen years of it, I've got the instruction down pat."

Neither Jonathan's nor Marisa's parents are grasping the power of positive expectations. If you expect the best of your child, you don't have to warn of punishment if he or she does the worst. And if you're expecting too much of your child (like Jonathan's parents are), you need to back off and examine why you're putting so much pressure on your kid. What dreams of your own are you trying to fulfill through your child?

7. Give Your Children Ownership of the Family

I often arrive at hotels late and hungry enough to eat the lobby brochures. At that point I'll even consider a restaurant that serves nothing but snack-sized peanuts and soft drinks.

"Is your restaurant still open?" I'll ask the reception clerk.

"No, it closes at ten o'clock."

"How about room service?"

"The kitchen closed at eleven."

I look at my watch; it's 11:03 p.m.

Now, if the manager of that hotel is smart, he or she will have empowered the person at the check-in desk to take charge of such situations. If a hotel hasn't done that, then I'll hear, "Sorry, there's nothing I can do about it."

But if the hotel manager is helping employees take ownership of the business and giving them freedom to make things happen, I'm more apt to hear, "Are you trying to find a full dinner?"

"No, ma'am. It's late. All I want is a sandwich."

"Well, let me see if I can talk to the cook before he leaves to put together a sandwich for you. Would that be okay?"

"That would be great."

Employees who care only for number one are thinking not about the business but about hightailing it out of there and getting home before *The Tonight Show with Jay Leno* comes on. Empowered employees are thinking about the hotel's reputation, about helping those who come through the doors. They take ownership of their work.

In a similar way, you can empower your children with your positive expectations to be responsible at home, at school, everywhere. You can prepare them a little at a time to first give back to the family, to be responsible and accountable at home. Rather than keeping your kids on a leash and doing everything yourself, **Kids who feel ownership will respect and give back to the family.** you let them take ownership of the family and the home.

Kids who feel ownership will respect and give back to the family. When friends or extended family come over, they'll do their part to pitch in and help. Home isn't a hotel in which the management (Dad and Mom) takes care of everything. And Mom isn't the slave dog who cleans up after them. Your kids will also learn quickly that not pitching in has consequences: loss of privileges to use the car, for instance, or to go out for the evening with friends.

Kids can do more things than you think: They can research movie showtimes, help plan the family camping trip, or map the vacation to see Grandma. The parent who delegates to instill a sense of ownership in her child is putting her positive expectations into action.

Most families are run autocratically. There's a king and a queen, and in a single-parent home, usually it's a queen. With this kind of organizational chart, it's easy to raise kids who don't care what happens to the castle, because they don't own it. They become takers, expecting the benevolent despots to do all the giving.

When I worked as a dean of students at the University of Arizona, we decided to expect the best of kids. We made paint available for them to decorate their dorm rooms and just charged them a little—maybe fifteen dollars—for the paint.

Did they graffiti their walls or toss cans from the dorm rooftops to create modern art on the sidewalk? No. They painted their rooms and took much better care of their living space because they'd invested in it.

If you give kids responsibility and ownership and expect them to do their part, more often than not, they will. That goes for home—and for school.

Back to School?

My wife and I had a stimulating conversation once about homeschooling.

"Honey," I said, "what do you think about homeschooling?"

"What?" she said.

And that was the end of that.

Some of you are homeschooling. You amaze me. I simply don't know how you do it. You're definitely organization geniuses, and you have a multitasking ability that far exceeds mine. In addition to the time it takes, homeschooling sets up other challenges. You can't exactly send a note to the teacher that says, "Oh well, Buford didn't get his homework done, since he slept in this morning." You have to get a little creative in your strategizing and in your discipline, don't you?

Whether you homeschool or send your kids to a public or private school, your attitude toward school will be a major part of your child's educational experience.

School is usually a child's first proving ground outside the home (even homeschooling has "groups" that get together outside the home)—and a major benchmark for parents' expectations. It segregates children according to age (or at least grade level), and then offers measures of performance based on below average, average, and above average. Whether this is wise isn't the point; it's what is done, and it tempts many parents to judge their own competence and identity according to how their children measure up.

A few weeks after sending out acceptance and rejection letters for the Massachusetts Institute of Technology's Class of 2006, Marilee Jones, dean of admissions, received a curt reply from a disgruntled father. Written on the dad's corporate letterhead, it read, "You rejected my son. He's devastated. See you in court."

Ironically, Marilee received another letter the very next day—this one from the man's son. It read: "Thank you for not admitting me to MIT. This is the best day of my life."[8]

Many parents are desperate not only to get their child's foot in the door at a prestigious school but to wrench that door off its hinges. "At MIT," said Jones, "we've been asked to return an application already in process so the parent can double-check his/her child's spelling. We've been sent daily faxes by parents with updates on their child's life. We've been asked by parents whether they should use their official letterhead when writing a letter of recommendation for their own child."[9]

But overinvolving yourself in your child's success or trying to railroad her into Harvard goes against the grain of raising a child to be responsible and thoughtful of others. Parents who complete their kid's college application (and I know many of them) are teaching a sad but clear lesson: "It doesn't matter how you play the game; it matters only whether you win or lose. You and I both know this is as much my application as yours, but character and integrity aren't as important as you getting in."

In doing so, you've essentially told your child that lying is okay and that you don't believe she has what it takes to make it on her own. Frankly, I'd rather send my children to Podunk Community College to study window washing than send them to Yale with that philosophy ringing in their ears! That only keeps them on the wheel, going round and round, trying to meet elusive expectations that they'll never be able to meet.

Think Way Back . . . to Kindergarten

This attitude of having to make your child a winner—instead of developing your child's character and responsibility—begins long before Junior or Missy goes off to college, though. It starts way back in kindergarten.

I'm amazed at the parents who treat even preschool with cut-throat seriousness. Last time I checked, the *pre* in *preschool* meant "*before* school." But many parents go nuts because their kids didn't get into the "right" preschool. This kind of attitude places inordinate pressure on children to stand out academically. It tempts them to cut corners and value achievement over character. And that pressure can hurt them all throughout their school years and into adulthood, because the weight of their parents' expectations is so great.

I always told my kids that I didn't expect perfect grades. I was more interested that they give everything their best shot. That 4.0 with a garnish of extracurricular activities may get your child into an

⊗ Keep an Eye on Your Critical Eye

What's your standard for behavior? Is it perfection? Is your goal to create a computerized mannequin that will do whatever you say as soon as you say it? If so, let me ask you a question: When was the last time *you* had a perfect day? When was the last twenty-four-hour stretch where you didn't utter a single cross word or respond a bit slowly to just one request? When have you maintained a positive attitude throughout the *entire* day?

Here are a few key points to remember:
- No one is perfect. (Not even you!)
- Training a child takes time.
- Getting a C isn't a crime.
- Sometimes "good enough" is, indeed, good enough.
- Love your child as he or she is . . . not as you *want* your child to be.
- Match your words to your actions. Don't redo a child's project so it'll be more perfect.

Ivy League school, but one day those grades will gather dust in boxes in the garage. But who will your child be? Ah, now *that* is what is most important in the long run. I guarantee that when she's thirty, no one is going to be asking her, "And what was your GPA in high school?"

The Pressure to Cheat

I walked into the kitchen one morning and found a piece of paper on the table on which Lauren had written:

Latin Test: Tuesday, May 20th

Conjugate verbs (that means put endings on them)

Suddenly, the years melted away. I caught myself reciting:

laudo (I praise)

laudas (you praise)

laudat (he praises)

laudamus (we praise)

laudant (they praise)

Lauren's note revived many (painful) memories for me. It took me five tries to pass Latin; even then I passed only because Carl Maahs was kind enough to lower his left shoulder.

Cheating my way through Latin cost me in two senses: Not only did I fail to learn the material, but I also didn't acquire study skills like discipline, teamwork, and creative thinking. (Well, maybe I exercised a bit of creative thinking, but not the kind you want to encourage.)

Unfortunately, too many other kids are like I was in school. Aaron Eisman, a high-school senior in an affluent Connecticut town, confessed that "In Westport, getting a B is like getting an F. So if you don't feel you can achieve it on your own, you find another way."[10] That "other way" for *three out of four* students these days includes cheating—from loading calculators with additional software to looking at a neighbor's test, as I did in Latin class.

Today's kids, driven to succeed from the day they dropped their diapers, need adults to step up to the plate and start stressing character and honesty over achievement with deception.

Dr. Suniya S. Luthar, a developmental psychologist at Teachers College at Columbia University, studies affluent teenagers like the ones in Westport. In this group, which she describes sympathetically as "a truly miserable group of kids," Dr. Luthar sees "higher rates of depression, anxiety, binge drinking and cheating . . . which she attributes to two causes: pressure to achieve and a lack of meaningful contact with adults."[11]

Lack of meaningful contact with adults. If that's not a cry for a family to focus on spending time with their kids, I don't know what is! Today's kids, driven to succeed from the day they dropped their diapers, need adults to step up to the plate and start stressing character and honesty over achievement with deception.

Grade the Grades

Occasionally during a conference, a parent approaches me and asks, "What should I do about my child whose grades aren't that great?"

"What kind of person is your child?" I'll ask.

"Oh, she's a great kid," the parent usually replies. "She's a caring sister."

"Does your kid obey you?"

"Sure."

"Wow," I'll say, "you're blessed to have a child like that."

"Well, Dr. Leman, we already knew that," the parent might respond, assuming I've missed the point of the question.

"Hear what I'm saying," I'll continue. "Your average thirteen-year-old makes a lot of choices in life. Today's teen is always within easy reach of drugs, sex, alcohol, shoplifting, vandalizing, you name it. Those things are all one step away. You must have done something right to raise a child who respects your values and thinks of others first. That says a lot more to me than whether her grade point average is 2.7 or 3.7."

Some parents have to stop and think at this point. "Yeah," they may admit, "we really are blessed to have the kid we do."

"You have to grade the grades," I add.

"Huh? What does that mean?"

"It means you need to put grades into perspective. Look at your kid's abilities, her level of dedication, her work ethic, and her life in general, and then grade the importance of her grades on that basis. I'd rather have a daughter who gets a B on a civics test, yet still sends thoughtful letters to her grandmother, than an obsessed student who gets an A+ in civics class but never talks to her grandparents because she thinks they're boring and they smell funny."

Am I lowering the bar too much by taking the focus away from grades? No. I hope we all have realistic expectations that call our children to grow in their gifts and abilities—and to do the best they can in school. But I don't see grades as the primary problem among kids today. Putting those grades in perspective—that's the issue that needs attention.

When was the last time someone asked to see your middle-school report card?

Just think: When was the last time someone asked to see your middle-school report card? How long has it been since someone asked for your high-school transcripts? How many years have passed since anyone mentioned the college you graduated from (or didn't graduate from)?

I have to confess, I'm a guy who, when questioned by his mom about why he got one C and four Fs on a midterm report card, said, "I dunno. I guess I just concentrated too hard on one subject." But did my lack of early academic success keep me from doing what I do today? Not at all! In fact, it's given me a lot of funny material!

If your child is getting the kind of grades I got growing up, tell him or her, "I'm sorry to see that you don't like school." But is your child learning? Does he like to take apart engines and find out what makes them work? Does she love to read Jane Austen novels on her own? Is he fascinated by movies, constantly borrowing your camcorder to direct his buddies in an amateur flick? I'm more concerned about whether my children are learning than I am about whether they're graduating in the top 10 or 20 percent of their class.

Likewise, when you see *good* grades on a report card, don't go playing college-placement officer. Don't say, "We're so proud of you—the colleges will be knocking down our front door to get you to come to their school!" Say instead, "It's great to see that you enjoy learning. I'll bet you're proud of those grades." Or "All that extra work you've done is really paying off!"

If your child is getting middle-of-the-road grades, and you honestly feel she's capable of doing better, ask what *she* thinks of her grades. She may admit she can do better. Then again, if she doesn't have the confidence to match her abilities, she may underestimate her potential.

No matter what schooling options you consider, just realize that it's important you don't take a thirteen-year leave of absence as soon as your child enters kindergarten and expect "the professionals" to take over. To evaluate how your child is doing academically, you need to know your child, know what she's learning, and know what the teacher is saying about her progress. If you're running from the office to the Chinese take-out counter for dinner, and then doing work on your laptop while you tuck the kids into bed, you won't have the inclination or peace of mind to keep track of how your kids are doing. Then, on the flip side, sometimes homeschooling parents struggle with knowing when to stop being a teacher and start being a parent.

When your child enters school, he needs your involvement now more than ever. If he senses that you've pulled away, that your house has become a hotel instead of a home, his school years will be harder than they have to be academically, socially, and emotionally.

Is It *Your* Homework?

You'll never hear me ask my kids, "Do you have homework?"

Why is that? Because they know whether they do, and my pesky reminders would only nag them to face something they should be facing themselves. If you've trained your children to be responsible all along the way, they will take ownership of their homework. Studying diligently is part of their responsibility.

I remember sitting down with one of our children and saying,

"Honey, these are *your* grades. I don't know why they send them to our house with your mother's and my name on them, because they're yours, but they do. And in nine months, some stranger whom you've never met is going to look at an eight-by-eleven-inch piece of paper with your name, your address, and these grades on it and make all sorts of assumptions about you. They don't know you like I know you; they don't see behind the figures. All they see is a name and a number. Now, understanding that, what do you think we should do about *your* grades?"

Your part is to help prepare a study area. Provide a desk and chair, and make sure the area is well lit. Let your child know that the desk isn't there for decorative purposes.

Many parents turn the living room into night school after the child has already done an hour of homework. Though school is very important, I'm not willing to turn my family's life upside down for school. When kids bring work home, make sure there are limits to the amount of time they spend on it. The PTA and the National Educational Association recommend the ten-minute rule: Take your child's grade level and multiply it by ten, and that's generally a good limit on how many minutes your child should be studying in the evening if homework is given (thirty minutes for a third grader, one hour for a sixth grader, etc.). If it takes more than that, there's a problem somewhere along the line.

But what if homework isn't getting done? Suppose you know that your eight-year-old son hasn't done his homework because you heard him in his room listening to a basketball game. Here's where reality discipline kicks in. You don't need to pester him ten times, saying, "Jehoshaphat, why aren't you doing your homework? How many times have I told you this evening to turn off that radio?"

Instead, don't say anything. Secretly call the teacher in the morning before class and say, "Mrs. McGillicuddy, I was just calling to let you know that Jehoshaphat didn't do a lick of homework last night."

Then the teacher can call him to the front of the classroom that morning and say, "Jehoshaphat, I was wondering if you would start off class by showing us the answers to our homework problems."

Having the teacher hold Jehoshaphat accountable for his actions is just helping reality discipline along a wee bit. You'll need to know your child, of course, to assess whether this will provide an appropriate jolt to his priorities. But even little Jehoshaphat can—and should—be held accountable for his actions by reality discipline. The "reality" is that he's responsible for getting his homework done on time; the "discipline" is the teacher calling him on the carpet—literally. If this is a pattern in your child, the brief injury to his ego will cost less in the long run than habitual irresponsibility.

There's another way in which kids need to take ownership of their school experience. I'm talking about the job of communicating what's going on at school. (This is also true of homeschoolers who go somewhere else for a separate class.)

On the way home from school one afternoon, Lauren talked excitedly about a mosaic they were creating in her classroom. She explained the process of creating its layers, and how it would take a couple of weeks to finish the whole thing. I'm not sure I understood it all. But that's why I'm a psychologist and not a mosaic artist.

I never ask my kids what they learned in school. Sooner or later they'll tell me about it, and it's healthier for them to initiate the conversation. Most young kids will tell you what they're thinking without your having to ask. And they'll tell you a lot more if you don't pester them. Pestering just slams their mouths shut.

So don't ask a young child, "What did you do in school, honey?" Young kids will answer, though if you ask them about it habitually, you've usually beaten that out of them by about fourth grade. Once they feel that answering your question is "reporting in," you won't get more than "nuthin'." If you set up a system in which you do all the questioning, kids learn over time to give rote responses.

"How was your day?"

"Fine." (Said as the kid is turned away from you, staring out the window.)

One mom I talked to didn't understand this. I turned to her husband and asked, "When you've finished an eight-hour day at work, how eager are you to go over every little detail of it with your wife? How does that sound?"

"Terrible!" he confessed. "I want to relax at home. The last thing I want to do is relive the very thing I'm trying to escape from."

"That's exactly my point!" I said. "Let your home be a home, a place of refuge, a place where your child can recover from the stresses of school rather than being forced to relive them."

Backward to the Future

In a society that pushes kids forward, you need to work hard at letting your children find their own pace. That's certainly true when it comes to education.

If your child isn't quite getting the coursework or doesn't seem to be as emotionally and socially mature as her classmates, and you're getting signals from the teacher to consider holding her back, don't get defensive. Don't yell, "Why do you say that about my daughter? She's very bright!"

No doubt she is. But intelligence and readiness are two different things. It doesn't take a PhD in psychology to realize that children mature at different rates. Unfortunately, most parents latch on to their child's school status as if the child's life depended on it.

Don't get me wrong. Just because I topped out in school with Ds, I'm not advocating a lower standard. But don't push your kids into the next grade if they aren't getting the material. If you're in doubt, hold them back. And if your child's teacher is in doubt, hold back on making a quick judgment.

It may seem traumatic now, but I guarantee that whether a boy or girl graduated from high school at eighteen or nineteen won't mean *anything* ten or even two years down the road. Can you imagine a company saying, "Well, we'd really like to promote Stan instead of Alice; he's better with people, more at ease with administration, and seems to have a better grasp of our company's business. But Alice was only sixteen when she graduated from high school, and Stan was nineteen. I guess we'll have to go with Alice."

That conversation will never happen. But let's say that Stan's parents decided to push him through school, even though he wasn't making it. Here's one scenario that might happen: "Stan seems to have the mind for this job, but he just doesn't have the confidence. And socially, I'm not sure he has what it takes to command others' respect. For that reason, I think Alice has the edge for this new position."

Your child's future employers will look at his or her character, social skills, and other abilities. They won't think to question how long it took your child to graduate from high school. All they'll care about is the *quality* of the person who emerged.

⊘ Take the Stress out of Schoolwork!

- Don't ask, "Do you have homework?"
- Don't turn home into a battle zone or a night class.
- Let reality be the teacher if your child doesn't finish homework.
- Get to know your child's teachers, in every arena (whether in private or public school or homeschool study groups).
- Don't do your child's homework. (After all, didn't you already go through fourth grade? Now it's your child's turn.)
- Support your school by going to meetings.

Our daughter Lauren was barely out of the starting blocks in school when we fired the gun again to start her over in kindergarten. Did holding her back a year mean that she was destined to forever lag behind? No. Did it damage her psyche because of a perceived failure? Hardly. Parents who read that into the situation are the ones who could have a negative impact in their child's life because of their hovering hypervigilance.

Today, Lauren is brighter than bright. She can literally recite the alphabet forward and backward and spell almost anything in English that comes her way. Lauren could very well be a published author by the time she's out of high school.

If you have siblings close in age, though, questions may be popping up in your mind. What happens when you have one child a year younger than the first? Are you going to hold your firstborn back a year, putting both children in the same grade? That's not a good idea, because you want to keep kids apart as much as possible.

If you have a child born in November, for example, and a second child born fifteen months later in February, make your decision with all kids in mind—and the more separation between the kids the better. If that firstborn November child is a little bluebird and your second-born February child is noticeably slow, you might put the firstborn in with kids his own age and then hold the second back a year. The gap would then be two years between them, which would help that second-born in particular. What you *wouldn't* want to do is push that slower-developing second-born child into the wake of that brainy little firstborn.

Getting the Teacher on Your Side

It's important to work well with your child's teachers. Maybe you can recite the introductory speech from PTA meetings and open houses. They say the same thing every year: "It's so nice to see par-

⊗ Take the Bite out of School

- Keep your parental ego out of your child's education.
- Focus on your child's learning, not on her grades.
- Let your child do his best, and accept that.
- Remember that test scores and class-placement stats can't measure every kind of ability.

ents here this evening working hand in hand with the school to broaden the horizons of the next generation."

The fact is, parents and teachers *don't* always work well together and are often at odds with one another. But when you feel the urge to take sides against your child's teacher, give that teacher the benefit of the doubt. If you hear from your child that the teacher did this or said that, don't call the principal—*call the teacher*. Go directly to the source.

Say, "Listen, I got this from a nine-year-old, but I want to get it from you. Here's what I heard happened in class today, but I want your take on it." Not only do you get the rest of the story, but your child learns that she can't mealy-mouth her way out of a situation by blaming someone else.

Having two children and a son-in-law who've worked in education, I've seen the system from all sides. It's natural for teachers to have a particular affinity for some students over others. We're all human; there are some personality types we get along with, and some we don't. But instead of making wild accusations of favoritism, try to understand what's getting in the way of your child and teacher having a productive relationship. Help the teacher understand your unique child.

This could be a valuable learning experience for your son or daughter, too. You might say something like this: "Honey, it's obvious that you and your teacher don't get along all that well. But I've spoken with him, and I believe he'll grade you fairly. You know, in one sense, this is a great opportunity to prepare you for the future. The day is going to come when you have a boss you might not get along with all that well either. But you're going to have to learn how to work in that person's company anyway, just like today you have to learn how to be a student in this teacher's classroom."

Your child's teacher may have as few as twenty students or as many as one hundred. It's not fair to expect her to immediately understand the best way to work with a kid you've known and loved for years. Get on your teacher's side, work with her, and your child will benefit.

Options Galore!

Seventeen-year-old Aaron Brown, a high-school student from Arlington, Texas, has been homeschooled most of his life, but recently he returned to school,[12] not a traditional public or private school, but something between those options and homeschooling.

Brown attends Grace Preparatory School, where he spends about fifteen to twenty hours each week in the classroom, or roughly half the time traditional public or private high-school students spend in class. The rest of his free time must be used for scheduling his own homework and study, which is exactly what will be expected of him in college.

This approach, known as university-model schooling (UMS), is a growing alternative to traditional public and private schooling, as well as homeschooling—and reflects the strengths of both.

In traditional public school, students typically spend thirty-five to forty hours per week in the classroom; homeschoolers, on the other hand, spend few, if any, hours in a formal classroom setting.

⊗ Which Schooling Option Is Best?

- Consider the personality and gifts of your child.
- Consider your own personality and gifts.
- Evaluate all schooling options for each of your children. (Not all children will flourish in the same type of environment.)
- Realize that schooling options may need to change as your child matures.

When the traditional student and the homeschooled student enter college and are expected to spend about fifteen credit hours per week in class and many more hours outside class, the transition requires significant adjustment—especially if the inner trait of discipline hasn't been adequately developed in a student.

UMS draws on the strength of traditional schooling in its preparation for the structured classroom experience in college, plus the parental involvement and encouragement of self-discipline that are hallmarks of homeschooling. It closely tracks with the aim of nurturing children from the inside out.

During early UMS elementary-school classes, parents are highly involved in instruction. They move gradually from the role of tutor to course monitor in the secondary-school years, when the number of classroom hours increases.

Like the homeschool model, UMS fosters character development and helps children grow in independence, while still allowing a high degree of parent-child interaction—your indelible imprint—along the way. I endorse UMS wholeheartedly for families looking for an option between traditional public/private schooling and homeschooling.

It continues to focus on parental nurturing that cultivates maturity and responsibility in children. "In 1992 psychotherapist Larry Shyers did a study while at the University of Florida in which he closely examined the behavior of 35 home schoolers and 35 public schoolers. He found that homeschoolers were generally more patient and less competitive. They tended to introduce themselves to one another more; they didn't fight as much. And the home schoolers were much more prone to exchange addresses and phone numbers. In short, they behaved like miniature adults."[13]

It's not my intention to advocate homeschooling over public schooling or private schooling over public schooling or any other combination. All have their merits and disadvantages. I simply want you to note a strength shared by homeschooled children: When a parent serves as the child's primary teacher, in school or in life, that parent has more influence. The child has a deeper understanding of who Mom and Dad are, and the interaction generally fosters deeper friendships between parent and child and an appreciation for the family's values.

Some critics of homeschooling warn that homeschoolers may not be "socialized" properly. I haven't found this to be a powerful argument. For starters, only in school are we segregated according to age. I've found homeschooled kids to be very adept at getting along with older children, younger children, and adults. They tend to be less cliquish and more mature in a variety of social settings.

Homeschoolers may also be less likely to get overly interested in the opposite sex at too young an age. When a child feels secure at home, he or she may not crave emotional validation from outside the home. It's uncommon to see homeschoolers pairing off in elementary or middle school—and that's a big plus in my book. Even middle schoolers are too young to form intense, emotionally involved, exclusive relationships with the opposite sex.

Having said all this, let me state that our children weren't homeschooled. They had some wonderful teachers, and we're thrilled with the experience they've had educationally. That's why I don't advocate one choice over the other. Each family needs to carefully choose what option is best. What works for one child may not work for every child, either. Keep the focus on the child's uniqueness.

No matter what schooling option you choose, though, the family should remain the center of your child's emotional world. You, Mom and Dad, need to stay in the driver's seat as your child's biggest influence and greatest inspiration at all times. Rooting your child's identity in your home and family is vital when facing the proving ground of school—or in moving anywhere in life.

Good Question!

How might you need to adjust your expectations of your child at home, at school, and in life?

The Top Ten Secrets for Successful Parents

- Be realistic with your expectations.
- Don't snowplow your child's road.
- Don't compare siblings.
- Play on your child's team.
- Don't harp on failures. Give your child grace.
- Allow your child's dreams to be *your child's* dreams . . . not yours.
- Think through schooling options carefully for *each child*.
- Never, ever do your child's homework.
- Form a team with your child's teachers to ensure the best education for your unique child.
- Always assume the best of your child.

NINE

THE BALANCING ACT

*How to walk that tightrope between work
and family without losing your balance.*

Let me ask you one very important question: What's your first thought when you get up in the morning? Do you say, "Wow, I can't wait to get going with my day. So many exciting things are happening!" Or do you groan, roll over, and hit the snooze button on your alarm . . . for the third time?

So many parents are living in burnout mode. They're exhausted critters, just like that gerbil on the wheel, running from place to place, from priority to priority, and by the time they land at home, there's little reserve left to give their families.

That's how Mark felt. In spite of his exhaustion and a nagging cold, he managed to make it to a weekend conference. Late on Saturday night, Stan, a man Mark respected, approached him.

"Can I be honest with you?" Stan asked.

"Sure," Mark replied.

"Okay, I see you as a guy who's strung out. You want to do everything well, and you're *trying* to do everything. But you can't; you'll burn out. How many hours per week do you work?"

"Probably fifty-five to sixty-five," Mark replied.

"You need to cut it to forty," Stan said.

"I don't know *anyone* who works only forty hours," Mark protested.

Stan, who owned his own company, replied, "Well, I don't know anyone who works more than forty. You just make it happen. Has Shelly ever talked to you about this?"

"Yeah, of course."

"Then don't wait until you're as old as I am to listen to your wife," said Stan.

Later Mark reflected, "When he had that conversation with me, it snapped me to attention. There were a few things converging in my life: that conversation, talking with my wife, Shelly, back at home, and a speech I heard that pointed out our lack of time to get everything done that we want. All of us have to 'cheat' someone out of the time we'd like to spend on them, and we tend to give our best to work or our hobbies, and cheat our family, who gets the leftovers."

Even after Mark and Shelly decided he would cut back, Mark didn't know if he could pull it off. "I had just turned in an aggressive budget for my work," he said. "If you're working sixty hours, and you suddenly cut back to forty, you're essentially cutting a part-time person from your office. But Stan peptalked me enough, and Shelly and I followed through with the decision. In the end, we believed he was right."

If you're never at home, how will you influence your children? And if you don't, who will?

If you're never at home, how will you influence your children? And if you don't, who will? Yes, I know. If you don't work, you can't afford to *buy* or rent a home, not to mention feed and clothe your family. But when your job overwhelms your family life, you need to bring your work back into balance. And you need to get yourself off the activity wheel for the sake of your own sanity—and for your family's sake.

How Important Is That Job Anyway?

Sometimes when I'm on the road thousands of miles from home, settling into my hotel for the weekend before speaking at a conference, I'll imagine what Sande and the kids are doing back in Tucson. I think, *What on earth am I doing here away from my family?*

Then I get home, peer in the mailbox, and see all the bills, and then I remember, *I'm making a living for my family.*

We might like to spend all our waking hours reading books with our kids, playing catch in the backyard, or going for family bike rides. But even though food grows on trees, the money to buy it doesn't. Unless your last name is Vanderbilt, Carnegie, or Rockefeller, you must earn a living for your family. Supporting that family both financially and emotionally can sometimes begin to feel like a circus juggling act.

Balancing these responsibilities is especially difficult in our overworked culture. The average American employee now works almost two thousand hours per year, which is over three hundred hours more than French workers, over four hundred hours more than German workers, and six hundred hours more than Norwegian workers. In every other industrial nation, the average number of hours worked per week is going down; only in developing nations, such as Malaysia, Sri Lanka, and Thailand, are the annual figures climbing along with those in the United States.[1]

For some companies, and some working parents, a kid is simply another ball in the air to juggle. But work must exist to support our families, not the other way around.

As trusted advisor to former President George W. Bush, Karen Hughes was arguably one of the most powerful women in America. Mark McKinnon, Bush's media adviser, estimated that President Bush turned to Hughes for twenty of the hundred big decisions he had to make every day. "He trusts her completely. He trusts her like he trusts no one," McKinnon said.[2]

But Hughes put her family first. She decided in spring 2002 to step down from her position so that she and her family could return to Texas—a choice that surely seemed madness to many.

One night late that March, Karen and husband, Jerry, and son, Robert, gathered around their kitchen table. "I really think we all want to go home to Texas," she said. She would later admit, "It was a relief for me to finally say it out loud."[3]

On April 17, following a meeting, Hughes asked chief of staff Andrew Card to leave without her. She had something to talk about with the president, who was getting ready to walk the dogs.

"Mr. President," she said when the two of them were alone, "I love you, but my family and I want to go back to Texas." They continued walking out of the White House and onto the manicured grounds as the president took in the stunning news.

"I know your family is a priority," he replied, "always have."[4]

No matter what your job, you must put your family relationships first. You may feel indispensable to your work, and colleagues may heap affirmation on you—affirmation you may not get at home. But there's no business more important than family. You may change jobs multiple times in your life. But your family deserves your devotion, focus, and single-minded care.

Don't Give It Your All

How often do you or your spouse get home from work, having given your all, with nothing left for your family? If we had annual performance reviews at home, many of us might be fired from our parenting responsibilities for failure to do our duty at home.

I suggest that breadwinners don't give their all to their work. If you pour 110 percent of your time and energy into pushing papers or training mechanics, what's left at home for pushing your kid on the swing and training your daughter to be a loving sister? If you give *everything* to your work, you won't have the emotional and physical resources to give your family what it needs.

If you give *everything* to your work, you won't have the emotional and physical resources to give your family what it needs.

It's not as though this world always rewards those who give their all at work, anyway. Gunther Cunningham, former head coach of the Kansas City Chiefs, was so dedicated to his job that the day after the season ended, he was still in his office at five in the morning—even though it was *Christmas Day*.

His reward?

He was fired two weeks later.

In my travels I've heard many heartbreaking tales of eager young women and men who put in long hours to make partner, get the corner office, become a VP, you name it, only to be dumped when someone who's willing to stay a little longer or play office politics a little better comes along. And what about those who fall victim to mergers, reorganizations, or downsizing?

Life is short, and kids are kids for such a short time. As much as I love my work, I want to be there for my kids' activities; I don't want to miss their special events, even if it means sitting on an emptier wallet or waking up in a smaller house.

How do you avoid giving your all to work?

First, *make quitting time as absolute as starting time*. You wouldn't show up for work an hour late; don't show up for home "late" either.

Second, *leave your work at work*. If you must take work home, resolve to do it only after the last child is in bed and your spouse is occupied with something else. You gave at least eight or nine hours to the office already; your family deserves your full attention for at least half that time.

Third, if your job is so stressful that you can't keep a decent schedule or avoid coming home wiped out, *get another job.*

"But it's not that easy!" you might say.

I never said it was. But your family's success is worth a good, hard effort, isn't it?

If your work is too demanding, find other work. That's putting it bluntly, and it may sound drastic. But what's the alternative? Well-fed, well-clothed, well-educated kids you never relate to?

Some organizations also ask employees to sacrifice by relocating. If yours asks you to move from Sante Fe to Seattle, and your extended family and friends are in Sante Fe, my vote is that you stay in Santa Fe at all reasonable costs. If you move to Seattle, you surrender a benefit no amount of money can compensate for: the relationships of grandparents, other relatives, and established friends. A healthy extended family is a lot to toss out the window for a few extra bucks and a new title on your business card.

Your priorities pave the way for your decisions—so get them straight. If your work exists to support your family, you'll be more apt to leave the office while others work late, and forgo promotions in favor of time together as a family. You'll tend to see work as a means, not an end.

I know from experience that it's hard to sit in a hotel room watching the Weather Channel when you'd rather be home watching the thunder-and-lightning storm with your kids over popcorn, comforting your little one, and oohing and aahing with the older ones.

Buy a Ticket to Your Child's Life

Lauren told me on the phone, long distance, that she was going to sing a solo in a school concert. I could tell from the excitement in her voice that she really wanted me to be there for her moment of glory.

⊗ Staying Connected While You're Away

When you have to be on the road, here are some great ways to stay connected to your kids' hearts:

- Call after school to see how their day went. (And no, texting won't
  do—your children need to hear your voice.)
- Leave special notes, one for each day you'll be gone.
- Keep bedtime routines intact, saying prayers or singing cherished
  songs together by phone.
- Record a reading of a favorite book so your child can listen to you
  "read on tape" before bedtime or during story time.
- Before you leave, agree on a special "reunion" activity . . . and stick to
  it like glue, no matter what work is waiting back in the office.

None of these are the same as being there in person, of course, but they
show your love—and make the reunion at home that much sweeter.

So I wiggled out of all kinds of work obligations and hurried
home from a trip so I could see her perform. It cost me a king's ran-
som to be there—nearly ten thousand dollars.

Arriving just in time, I walked into the school auditorium expecting to see rows of squirming, jabbering kids. But no one was
there.

Had I gotten the time wrong?

I hustled to the school office. "What happened to the school
concert?" I asked.

"What concert?" the woman replied. "I don't know of any school
concert. Why don't you check your daughter's classroom?"

I set off down the hallway. Reaching Lauren's second-grade
room, I entered . . . just as my daughter delivered her six-word solo
in a little class play.

That was the "concert." The cost of getting there made for the highest-priced ticket I've ever bought for any event—but I was there!

You know what? It was worth it. When I saw Lauren's face light up as I walked into the room, I realized I hadn't bought just an expensive plane ticket; I'd purchased a memory with my daughter that may last a lifetime. Even if she forgets this event—though I doubt she will—she'll still know that when it really mattered, I was there.

I hadn't bought just an expensive plane ticket; I'd purchased a memory with my daughter that may last a lifetime.

I hear business moguls talk all the time about marketing their products. Well, how about marketing our love to our kids? While Madison Avenue seeks to sell them jeans, perfume, and the latest DVDs, let's advertise our interest, our commitment, and our involvement.

In business terms, that's what I was doing: marketing my concern and my devotion to Lauren. The money I spent on my "marketing campaign" could have purchased a full-page ad in our local newspaper, but this wasn't a one-day sale. It was a lifetime memory. I wasn't peddling a better mousetrap; I was proclaiming my love and commitment to my precious little daughter.

I know guys who drop four hundred bucks to buy the latest titanium driver, and all that does is put their little white golf ball a few yards farther out of bounds! Yet those same dads balk at the thought of parting with half that much money to be at an important event in their children's lives.

Make no mistake: There are costs to pay when balancing work and family. Some parents will refuse higher-paying promotions because the time and travel would take too much. Others will go to work earlier so they can return home before their kids get back from school. Still others will sacrifice years of work or give up their careers altogether to focus on their children.

I'm not pretending the cost isn't real or significant. I'm admitting that, *yes*, parenting will ask you to sacrifice. I ought to know. As a working dad, I live with this reality every day.

But I'm also saying that the costs and sacrifice are worth it. They're the absolute best investment you can ever make.

The Homestretch Home

If you're going to sacrifice to gain family time, you may as well make it quality time. That means making the transition from your workday to home in a way that doesn't leave you wrung out. Not every commute home from work is filled with relaxed thoughts and a deep reservoir of energy to give kids. I know what that feels like.

You've had a hectic day. As you drive through traffic, you need a restroom like you've never needed anything else. For the last seven miles, you've even considered making use of the empty soda bottle one of your kids left in the car, but you figure you can make it to your house.

When this happens, call your spouse on the cell phone and say, "Honey, I'm five minutes away, but when I get home, I really need to go potty. I'm about to bust a bladder. Just give me three minutes." Win the pledge of your mate and kids not to pounce on you right away.

Next, prepare your mind. Maybe you love listening to political discussions heating up talk radio on the drive home, or keeping in touch with Wall Street's ups and downs at the market's close. Instead, choose a different station, something that soothes you, like soft elevator music (okay, I saw that eye roll you just did) or oldies.

Maybe when you get home you love to check the mail and peruse the newspaper. Decide instead not to go through either right away. (To keep a future visit to the urologist at bay, however, accept that when you get home, you really *should* go potty.)

Finally, realize that although you're exhausted, the kids have already been home a few hours, and they probably want a little piece of you. If you're smart, you'll give it to them. After they've had their fill, they'll go away and leave you to hyperventilate and finally change clothes.

Loving your kids means communicating, *I love you more than this briefcase, more than that newspaper sitting on the coffee table, and certainly more than that stack of bills sitting on the counter.* Those first seconds as you walk through the door (or after your potty break) set the tone of your time with your children.

Imagine what a gift it is to them when you demonstrate the message, *I'm so happy to see you!*

Give Parenting Your Best Shot

Remember Mark, whose fifty-five to sixty-five hours each week at the office were taking their toll on his energy and ability to be present with his wife and two kids?

"It wasn't just a lack of time," he said. "I was wiped out when I got home."

After talking with Stan, Mark approached his boss as they walked out of a meeting. "I just want you to know I'm cutting back on my hours," Mark said. "I'm not going to work sixty hours a week anymore. I'm not sure what's going to happen to my numbers and profitability, but it's what I have to do."

"Well," his boss replied, "there are times when you have to work those kind of hours."

"I understand that there *are* those times," Mark replied, "but I'm not going to do it anymore."

Mark and Shelly waited to see what would happen.

Not only did the office end up making its budget; it won awards for its work besides!

"The turnaround was amazing when I had more time and energy for my family," Mark said later. "I also have a lot more to give Shelly. All around, it was a wise decision."

Yes, deciding to keep your heart, your time, and your focus at home does mean sacrifices. But it also provides the most stable foundation on which you can build your life—and often results in rewards that are bigger than anything you gave up.

Many women and men have found they can do much more working forty hours a week and getting their batteries recharged at home than they can putting in sixty-hour weeks and being depressed, anxious, and tired.

This is your child. Nobody else will love her like you do.

You have one shot at parenting, so why not give it your best shot?

This is your child. Nobody else will love her like you do. She may not have come at a convenient time. Careerwise, she might represent a big hiccup to your advancement. You may not be financially ready. But she's here. What are you going to do about it?

It's not as if you can put her on hold for eighteen years until you're more financially secure and your vocation has calmed down a bit. Every second of their lives, our children march ever further down the road of independence—and they rarely go backward. A baby will stay in your arms all day long; a two-year-old will take only so much cuddle time before she wants down to run. And a teenager? Well, you're lucky to track him down between texting, school plays, and pizza nights out.

If you don't slow down for these important parenting years, when will you? The person who spends the most time with your child—especially in those first six years of life—is the person who will most influence her development. Her surroundings will have a major impact on her values, beliefs, and attitudes. So are you going to be there for her, helping create a healthy, well-balanced environment, so she can have a healthy, well-balanced outlook on life?

Every sacrifice and tough decision you make will be worth it in the end. You're the one in charge, so you need to do what's best for your family.

And no one knows your child better than you.

To Work or Not to Work (Outside the Home)?

This next section is especially for you moms, since you're the ones most likely to be thinking about whether to stay home with your child.

Not long ago, while killing time at the airport in Atlanta, waiting for my flight to Buffalo, New York, I sat down next to a poster-material blonde baby and her very Italian-looking mother. I could tell the mother was nervous, thinking, *Oh no, now I've got to keep the baby especially quiet. This guy's old enough to be a grandpa, but what if the kid starts to fuss?*

To set the mother at ease right away, I said with a grin, "Lucky me. I get to sit next to such a cute baby. She's adorable! I love babies! I've had five myself. And now the youngest is ten, and the oldest is thirty. Time sure does fly."

The mother visibly relaxed. As we waited for the boarding call, the mother confessed that she really didn't want to have kids, because her career was going well. "Then Anne came along"—she gestured toward her daughter—"and, well, I fell in love. With my daughter. And suddenly the choice that I had been wrestling over since I found out I was pregnant—to work or not to work—wasn't so difficult anymore."

Women today have more career choices than ever before, but along with those choices comes the difficult decision of whether to pursue an outside-the-home career. And if they work, do they work full-time in an office, full-time from home, part-time from the office, part-time from home, or a few hours a week? Or do they put their career on hold until their child is in kindergarten or be a stay-at-home mom? The options are dizzying.

Awhile back, Larry King was interviewing Dr. Brenda Hunter, author of *Home by Choice*. At the time, King was facing the birth of another child.

"Dr. Hunter," he asked, "does it really matter whose arms hold the child?"

Her answer, well researched in her book, was a definitive yes.

It does matter whose arms are holding the child. As the old gospel song reminds us, "The arm bone's connected to the shoulder bone; the shoulder bone's connected to the neck bone; the neck bone's connected to the head bone."[5] And the head bone surrounds the brain, which is the center of your value system.

If you drop off your bleary-eyed two-year-old at day care around 6:30 a.m., pick him up at 6:30 p.m., and put him to bed two hours later, who's teaching your child about life? Is it someone who's getting paid just above minimum wage, who two months ago decided to work at a day-care center because she grew bored with folding clothes in the women's department of a store at the mall?

> **What good does it do to have a child reading when she's three years old if she never calls home when she's thirty?**

In institutional day care, your child may acquire the academic and social skills to "make the grade." But is that all you want from the new life you've introduced into the world? What good does it do to have a child reading when she's three years old if she never calls home when she's thirty? Is that a good trade?

Some folks believe that it doesn't really matter whether a child grows up in day care or grows up at home.[6] But in your heart of hearts, you know better, don't you? Will your child run pell-mell into the arms of a day-care worker the way she runs into your arms when she sees you?

"I was once on the old *Donahue* show," said Dr. Laura Schlessinger, "being interviewed by him about [my book] *Ten Stupid Things Women Do to Mess Up Their Lives*, and even though there was nothing in there about daycare, they had, according to an audience member, stocked the audience with young feminist females to attack me, to make it controversial, to make it an interesting show. . . . I got pretty irritated with the audience after a while and I said, 'OK, tell you what, if you could die and be recycled and come back as a infant, stand up if you would rather be raised by a daycare worker, a nanny, or a babysitter. Stand up now.'

"And, you know, in this whole audience that was attacking me like crazy, nobody stood up. The camera panned back—I have a tape of this, because every now and then I like to watch it—and nobody moved. So I said, 'Then why are you going to do this to your children?'"[7]

Most of us don't want anyone but our parents raising us. Yet many of us want to assuage our guilt for handing our kids over to day-care workers. The blunt truth is that you can't have it both ways. If you want your children to receive maximum benefit from your parenting, childcare outside the home is simply not the best option.

One of the most publicized findings of the National Institute of Child Health and Human Development's (NICHD) Early Child Research Network reported that as children ages three months to four years spent more hours in nonmaternal childcare (anyone except the mother), their levels of disobedience and aggression in kindergarten escalated, according to their teachers.[8]

Some will point out that these behaviors were within normal ranges, meaning they weren't serious enough to require intervention. I believe, however, that the point still stands: Institutional day care is not as good a choice as full-time care by the child's mother or father.

Another study found that stress levels in toddlers (ages sixteen to thirty-eight months) increased over the course of a day at a day-care center, especially when compared to infants. On days at home, stress levels decreased as the day progressed.[9]

What Are Your Options?

Most companies today will grant you a few months of maternity leave and a month or so of paternity leave. But they generally expect you to find a day-care center or nanny and punch back into work well before your baby has blessed you with his first laugh.

Because you fear losing your job or the career momentum you had before the baby arrived, you cut a few corners. *After all,* you tell yourself, *he sleeps half the day anyway. It's not like I'm really gone from him for ten hours—he's sleeping three or four of them, so those don't count!* So you return to work a few days early, just to show your boss you're a "team player."

This can produce what I call "Kiddie Kennel Kids"—children who spend almost all their waking hours in day care throughout their preschool years. Their parents drop them off at 6:30 a.m. on the way to work and pick them up at 6:30 p.m. on the way home. They'll grow up not knowing anything different.

If this is true of your child, I want to ask you something: Are you doing this for your child's benefit or for yours?

I realize that you may not have the option of staying home, especially if you're the sole breadwinner in your family. If you're doing it because you think preschool is a must, though, please think again. Preschool is all right as long as it's not overdone, but it certainly isn't necessary. I didn't go. Has that stopped you from reading this book? Is there a disclaimer on the cover that says, "By the way, Dr. Leman didn't go to preschool when he was three years old"?

If you've determined that preschool is best for your child, a three-year-old can usually handle two-and-a-half hours a day, three times a week. But no two-year-old belongs in preschool. There's no "schooling" going on there; it's just babysitting by another name.

If after reviewing your options, you decide that someone else must watch your child, consider a babysitting co-op. It has at least three advantages: Its cost is negligible or nonexistent; it allows your child to receive some of the socialization that can be a strength of preschools and day-care centers; and when it's your turn to help with the co-op, it lets you see your child interacting with other children.

If you're organizing the co-op yourself, you can choose those who are involved, which promotes shared values. The low cost may free up money in your budget, allowing you to remain home for more hours. And the quality of care and concern is likely to be higher.

For others, institutional childcare may be necessary. If your child is at a day-care facility, ask yourself these questions:

- Would you want to be there?
- Is it clean?
- Can you show up at any time?
- How do the teachers interact with the children?
- Does the program align with your values?

I know it's not popular to suggest that some people, in their present circumstances, are not able to give their children what's best for them. It's not my intention to add insult to injury. Do the best you can with what you have, making changes as you're able, with the goal of spending as much time with your kids as possible.

Consider, too, how your kids will someday view the childcare choices you make today. In time, most children will come to appreciate your efforts to do the best you could with what you had; they'll have difficulty, however, if you *chose* to make work a priority over a relationship with them.

All your son or daughter will know is how much time, effort, and sacrifice you seemed to make for his or her sake. I've sat in too many counseling rooms not to know that your kids will see time spent in day care as *their* sacrifice, not yours. You may think you're working extra hours for them, but they won't see it that way.

On the other hand, I've never seen a kid resent the fact that one of his or her parents stayed home. Children always view that as a great gift and a clear sign of their parents' commitment to them.

Think of your best childhood memories. Go ahead and take a minute. I'll wait . . .

Some of my best memories include playing outside on a cold November day in Buffalo, New York, throwing rocks into the neighbor's goldfish pond, or playing with my trucks, moving sand around in the sandbox. But you know an even better memory? Hearing my mother call me in for lunch and serving me warm tomato soup with cheese sandwiches. Mom always put butter on the top of my tomato soup—I can still visualize that creamy butter spreading out and covering my soup. I just loved the way it tasted!

One day Mom seemed a bit rushed, so she asked me if I thought I could make my own soup and sandwiches. I told her with a straight face, "Well, I suppose I could, but it sure tastes better when you make it, Mom."

That's all she needed to hear. She set aside what she was doing and made me a lunch I'll never forget.

I've eaten a lot of lunches in my sixty-plus years. How many of those can I remember? Not very many. But I remember that one lunch because it holds very warm feelings connected with my mom.

Twenty years down the road, when someone asks your child about his childhood, will he talk about the childcare worker who bandaged his knee? Will he talk about being tied into a line as he and fifteen other two-year-olds walked to the park with the Worker of the Month?

Or will he talk about autumn afternoons drinking a cup of hot chocolate while Mommy read him his favorite book? Will he laugh about the wagon rides you gave him on the way to the grocery store to pick up a gallon of milk?

It's all in the perspective.

And the most important years of all are the first six years.

The First Six Years

One of the most common questions I hear on the road is this: "Dr. Leman, I'd really like to return to my job, but I don't want to short-change my child. How long should a mother stay at home before going back to work if she really wants to put her child's development first?"

"Are you asking me what is truly best for your child?" I'll ask.

"Yes," she'll say, expecting me to say something shocking—like six months.

"Then I recommend you stay home the first six *years* of your child's life. You may consider that a tall order, but when you think about it against the sweep of your life, it isn't much more than taking time off for college. Eighty percent of your child's personality is formed by age four, so if you can remain home during those formative years, so much the better. By age six, your child is starting school, and the transition back to work—if you choose to return—will be a natural one."

"But no company will hold my job that long!" the woman might protest.

"I realize that, but that's not what you asked me. You asked me what was truly best for your child, and that's the question I answered. I believe every child deserves a full-time mom for the first six years of his or her life."

Now stop right there, Dr. Leman, some of you are saying. *No way can I afford to stay home with my child that long.*

But have you thought through what you would gain?

When you're willing to sacrifice, you'll learn how to do without some privileges and quite a few extra possessions. When Holly was born, Sande and I owned just one car. Both of us grew up in a two-car family, and everybody we knew owned two cars, but we couldn't afford it because we had both agreed on Sande staying home with the kids.

Because of the challenges we faced during these years, I know the fear of living with expenses that always seem greater than your income. I know exactly what it feels like to have to choose between buying milk or laundry detergent on any given shopping trip. I had three young children and made just $22,000 a year. When we got a letter announcing that the mortgage payment on our house was going up from $188 to $212 a month, I just about died. I can still remember holding that letter in my hand thinking, *How are we going to handle this?*

But never did we question our decision to keep Sande home. When we first got married, Sande worked as a service rep for Ma Bell; then she quit when Holly was born. Once the kids were in school, Sande became a preschool teacher so she could be there when the kids got home and still help out with our family income.

There were many humbling moments during those years. We didn't buy many clothes but gratefully accepted the hand-me-downs that had a way of showing up on our doorstep or in our living room. Our big treat was to go to a cafeteria where our family of five ate for less than fifteen dollars.

Because we had just one car and I had to drive it to work, Sande's big outing was when my dad would pick her and the kids up and take them to Sambo's Restaurant, home of the ten-cent cup of coffee.

Living on one income was a sacrifice, but we got through it. And you know what? We wouldn't change a thing. We've now enjoyed four decades of being very close as a family.

Should I Work—or Not?

- Consider your own energy level and the impact working will have on it.
- Adjust for the age, stage, needs, and personality of your particular child.
- Evaluate your real motivation for wanting to work.
- Be aware of the hidden costs of full-time or part-time childcare outside the home.
- Recognize the hidden costs of working outside the home (gas for your car, a new wardrobe that doesn't feature baby spit-up).

Do you think our kids would still want to get together if home life had been rushed, harried, and so broken up with multiple activities that we barely had time to get to know one another? The last thing a working mom has in the morning is unhurried time, and the last thing she has in the evening is energy. As a result, a child usually gets shortchanged on both ends. For Sande and for me, the sacrifices we made at the time were so small in light of the rewards we enjoy today as a result.

So, parent, anything you can do to put your children first—as you balance home and work—will be more than worth it.

Is It Flex Time Yet?

Thankfully, some companies have embraced all sorts of arrangements to accommodate families—such as sequencing, job sharing, part-time work, telecommuting, and flex scheduling.

I talk with a lot of flight attendants in my travels, and some have arrangements with the airline that allow them to work only a couple of days every two weeks. These attendants figure they can find quality care—Grandma, a sister, or a close friend who's also a mom—for their kids during those two days, and they still get to keep their jobs and reduced-cost flight privileges to visit other family members.

When my assistant had a daughter at home, my office hours were 7:00 a.m. to 3:00 p.m. Why? The "inconvenience" to an organization that wanted to reach me at 4:00 p.m. didn't matter half as much to me as the inconvenience to an adolescent who'd otherwise come home from school to an empty house.

Some families who strive for the home-court advantage make other choices for the sake of their kids. They may move closer to work to facilitate a shorter commute, downsize their monthly rent or mortgage, or even take a cut in pay.

So let me ask you this question: Are you doing the best right now with the time and money you have? If you're still deciding whether to work outside the home, make sure you have all the facts first.

Counting the Cost

If you're considering going back to work—or are currently working and want to reconsider staying at home—first count the cost:

1. *Ask yourself, What am I working for? Why do I do what I do?* You may have multiple reasons, but if few of your motivations include family, that may indicate that work has a greater hold on you than it should.

2. *Calculate how much returning to work will add to your income.* Don't forget to subtract the cost of childcare, taxes, clothes you'll need to buy for work, meals out, transportation to and from work (perhaps including the cost of using an extra car), housecleaning, and so on.

    Do the math. Is returning to work worth it? You might want to first calculate what you need to earn in order to pay for the childcare.[10] Often a better option is to cut back on your expenses rather than sending another parent to work to maintain your current lifestyle. A sacrifice in terms of where or how you live may spell the difference between one parent or both parents working.

3. *Ask yourself, "How long do I need to stick to the plan to stay at home?"* We're not talking about tightening your belt for the rest of your lives. Tight budgeting for a little longer than it takes to get a college degree is well worth it to have children who receive the nurturing, love, and attention they need from one of their parents during the day. Of course, if you have three children, that college degree could become a PhD. Even so, ten years still represents a fraction of an adult's life—but more than half of your child's.

4. *Explore work-from-home alternatives or split scheduling.* If you truly must work, try to find something that allows you to have at least one parent home whenever the kids are out of school (but make sure the two of you have sufficient time together so that you can maintain your marriage). Consider taking a part-time job during school hours, even if the pay is less.

5. *Finally, be brave enough to ask your son or daughter about your decision to return to work.* Shoot straight. Ask your child, "Honey, what do you think about Mommy going back to work?" Your child's response just might help with your decision.

Every Mom Is a Working Mom

"You were slated to become the first female black astronaut, yet you gave it up," host Sally Jessy Raphael challenged Helen Jackson on her daytime talk show. "Why?"

"My oldest son was having trouble in school," replied Helen, who had returned to work when Malik was three weeks old. "He was severely withdrawn and depressed. He had failed sixth grade. My son was fast becoming a statistic."[11]

You may have seen the bumper sticker that reads, "Every mother is a working mother." It's true. Whether or not a mother works outside the home following the birth of her child, she's got plenty of work to do.

> **You may have seen the bumper sticker that reads, "Every mother is a working mother." It's true.**

But in recent years that truth hasn't gotten much respect. However, all studies show that having Mom at home is particularly important—and better for the entire family. Consider that the previously mentioned results of the study by the Early Child Care Research Network hinged on the *mother's* involvement with the child.

To opt out of working outside the home, however, a mother needs options. Unfortunately, many families' lifestyles create a demand that can't be met unless both parents work outside the home. If possible, don't let finances dictate your decision.

"So Helen [Jackson] came home and began homeschooling her three older children," wrote Dr. Brenda Hunter in her book *Home by Choice*. "After only nine months of homeschooling, all three children had soared by two or more grade levels in all academic areas. Malik, who had previously performed at the fourth grade level, now tested at the ninth grade level. No longer withdrawn and depressed, he began to develop socially and in time became a leader among his friends at church."[12]

" 'I'm not sorry that I gave up my career,' Helen added. 'Sure, I was doing my thing, but my kids were suffering. And I could never feel good if my children were unhappy.' "[13]

Instead of exploring space, Helen set out to explore her children's potential—a decision she *and* her children will no doubt look back on with gratitude.

Fathers: Wired to Nurture

"One of my first memories growing up was wishing my father would be home more," reflected Dr. Andrew Hudnut, a family physician from Sacramento, California. "I was 8, and we had just returned from a canoe trip. I remember thinking, 'I don't want a bigger house or more money. I just want my dad around.'"[14]

Thankfully, more and more fathers are willing to sacrifice to gain that home-court advantage with their children:

In a national survey developed by the Radcliffe Public Policy Center at Harvard, 82 percent of men in their 20s and 30s said that things like salary and prestige aren't as important in a job as whether it'll allow them time with their family. Increasingly, employers appear to be listening. Three in four businesses surveyed by consulting firm Hewitt Associates said they offer such alternatives as part-time, flextime, job sharing, telecommuting, or a compressed week of longer workdays swapped for a day off. That's a 45 percent jump in ten years.[15]

The inner drive of fathers to return to the nest and nurture their children isn't only emotional. Research shows that in the weeks around the birth of a child, fathers show higher levels of estrogen and a rise in prolactin, the hormone that aids in a woman's lactation. There's also a 33 percent decrease in testosterone the first three weeks after the birth.[16] Why? The best guess is that "women's hormone levels are timed to the birth—and men's hormone levels are tied to their partners," says psychologist Anne Storey.[17]

Which means, Dad, that the stirrings to invest in your children are wired into your nature from the moment your child arrives.

So are yours, Mom.

If you listen to them, you'll get yourself off the activity wheel and into a more stable home environment, with more time with your children.

And you'll also experience those rare moments when the highest success you could earn in your career won't hold a candle to your child's smile and hearing him or her say, "I love you!"

But What If I'm a Single Parent?

For those of you in the trenches, there's not a tougher job in the world than being a single parent. You don't have the luxury of staying home without working—and you're constantly under pressure (and feeling guilty because your child doesn't have two parents). What you lack most are help and time. You can't buy time, so you can only come up with creative ways to free up more of your time.

Some single moms will tell you they'd be thrilled to go potty by themselves in peace and quiet. For many, having part of a day each week that they can call their own happens only in their dreams.

Single mom, I know you feel that life has kicked you in the teeth. I know you didn't expect your husband to die, or ask you for a divorce.

Single dad, I know you didn't want to hear from your friend that he saw your wife with another man.

Nor did your kids wish for any of these scenarios. Now everybody's paying for it.

The question to ask yourself is not "What did I do to deserve this?" but "What am I going to do with the path ahead?"

The question to ask yourself is not *What did I do to deserve this?* but *What am I going to do with the path ahead?*

Parenting solo is challenging, but you and your kids can still finish strong if you give them the discipline they need; a predictable, safe environment; a healthy dose of vitamin N (saying no) and vitamin E (encouragement); and the wise use of the time you *do* have.

Unfortunately, guilt often motivates the child-rearing decisions of single parents. They see what other families have and stretch themselves thin trying to keep up. They neglect their own health for the sake of their kids' schedules. They play the if-only game—*if only* he hadn't cheated on me, *if only* I hadn't gotten pregnant out of wedlock, *if only* I'd gotten that job I interviewed for.

Often the kids make things worse. They point out that they don't have the things other kids do, making Mom or Dad feel even more guilty.

Because of that guilt, and because single parents aren't able to be home as much, it's easy for them to fall into the activity trap. Or they may have such demanding schedules that when they get time away from work, they'll do almost anything to get a break. If you're tempted in either of these directions, be careful: There are too many harmful influences seducing your child for you to go on autopilot. Value your time together as gold. And protect it as you would a treasure stash.

Ten Practical Strategies for Low-Cost Survival

Single parents, of all people, need and deserve some time for themselves. But to get it, you have to be creative. The following strategies will help.

1. Organize a babysitting co-op. I know I mentioned this before, but it's an idea that works wonders in giving you some freedom. Organizing a group of friends or other parents (single or married) for this purpose is one of the most practical, helpful ways to barter time without cost. Those hours away from your child one morning or afternoon a week will let you get housework done or relax in the tub or read a book—all without putting your child in preschool.

2. Connect with other families in your community. Sometimes you have to tell people what your needs are, which isn't always a comfortable thing to do. You might approach a couple you know from your place of worship, your child's school, or your son's Cub Scout troop,

✍ Creative Day Care for Single Parents

- Consider asking a family member or close friend to watch your kids during the day. (Chances are, they already know and love your child, and that's better than a day-care worker who doesn't.)
- Even better, have Grandma or Grandpa come to your home and help out. (Even if they can only come one day a week, your child has the added benefit of being home, your child's favorite place.)
- Check out a church-run facility.
- Consider starting your own at-home business so you can take care of your child at home.

and say, for example, "I know you fish a lot. Is there any way you could take my son fishing with you? I'm not much of a fisherman; I don't even know a hook from a line."

If you *aren't* a single parent, look around for the single moms and dads who would value your help. Consider offering to take care of a child for an afternoon so that a single parent has a little breathing room.

3. Hang in there by hanging together. Children of single parents learn quickly that everybody pitches in—for instance, by age eight or nine when they come home from school, they have to take food out of the freezer in preparation for dinner. That mentality of "It's you and me, kid, against the world" can foster intimacy between a single parent and his or her child, as well as develop emotional fortitude and responsibility.

4. Be consistent in your discipline. Since single parents are under extra stress and are tired more often than not, you're likely to respond to circumstances based on your level of exhaustion. Sometimes you'll let a bout of sassing go unheeded, only to "drop the hammer" on the same offense two days later.

Though it's incredibly difficult to never have a relief pitcher, consistency is a must for children's stability and psychological development. In a calm moment, sit down and decide what your expectations will be, make those expectations known to your children, and then enforce them. That may also mean allowing little things (elbows on the table or an occasional belch) to go uncommented on as you focus on what's most important.

5. *Don't let guilt run your life.* The problem with guilt is that it cements you to the past. You can't undo life, so focus on the present and the future.

Just because your or your spouse's actions may have put your kids in a less-than-ideal situation, it doesn't mean they should get a toy you can't afford. It also doesn't mean they can avoid chores or dress inappropriately. What happened, happened; do your best to deal with the here and now.

6. *Start telling people you love that you need help.* This includes parents, sisters or brothers, and trusted friends. Kids were never meant to be raised alone. Though you may not have a husband or wife, look for a grandparent, a sibling, or even a close friend to assist you.

7. *Make meals in quantity.* With a group of friends, family members, or neighborhood mothers—even by yourself—fix thirty days' worth of meals to freeze for later use. Dinners with your kids are one of the best ways for families to interact, and this tip can make those times more hassle-free.

If you're preparing meals as a group, each person should bring a tasty, inexpensive recipe and the necessary ingredients. The group then makes a bulk batch of each recipe, which is divided up among everyone to take home. Or have people make the meal in bulk at home, multiplying the quantity for others in the group; then when you meet, simply swap meals to take home and freeze. If your children are old enough, do this with them. You might set aside the first Saturday of every month as your making-meals day, for example. Your kids will have a blast doing it with you, and you'll be spending quantity and quality time with them.

8. Take advantage of free activities. There are plenty of free things single parents can do with their kids. Try story time at the library or bookstore (which may allow you to read on your own or simply have some quiet time), visits to parks, outdoor concerts, and so on.

9. Suggest useful gifts. When people ask what they can give you for birthdays or Christmas, be practical: "I'd love a gift certificate for three hours of housecleaning from Merry Maids," or "We'd love a gift certificate to Applebee's." These gifts give you more time together as a family by freeing you from chores.

10. Let grandparents be grandparents. But keep parenting in your court. Single parents are sometimes so exhausted that they allow grandparents to become de facto parents. But don't let anyone assume your role as parent.

Here's an example: Rachel, a single mom, was going to move in with her parents after her divorce just until she got back on her feet. Now she's been there six years, and her oldest child is eleven. Last Christmas, Grandma and Grandpa surprised the family with a gift: "We're all going to Disneyland!"

The grandparents might have thought they were doing everyone a favor, but it would have been better to make the reservation for the grandkids and daughter, and let *her* take the kids to Disneyland.

Why? Because Rachel was becoming her parents' little girl again—in essence, an older sibling to her own children.

No matter the stresses in your life right now, don't ever surrender your role as parent. Make sure that you remain in the driver's seat of your child's life.

Your kids need you too much, and they deserve a mom or dad who is connected with them as much as possible. No other people or activities can take your place.

That's how important you are to your kids.

Good Question!

What steps will you take in the next month to put your family first? (My guess is that you'll never want to go back to the way you've been living once you experience the rewards!)

Focus on the Family . . . First

- You may *feel* indispensable to your work, but you *are* indispensable to your family. Don't give your all at work; save time and energy for your kids.
- Choose your work commitments wisely. If you're asked to relocate, stay put if at all possible, especially if you'd be leaving extended family. If your work is too demanding, find a different job.
- Advertise your interest, commitment, and love to your kids by spending time with them—even if it costs you money.
- Use your commute home from work to prepare yourself to spend quality time with your family.
- Before you increase your work hours, see what needs and wants can be trimmed at home first. What your kids need most is your time and attention.

TEN

YOU CAN DO IT!

*How to transition to a better way of life
without too much Fish-Out-of-Water Syndrome.*

As a child, I spent most of my time fishing in Ellicott Creek. And those carefree days taught me that when fish are hooked, they sometimes do something odd—they take to the air. A fish will occasionally break the water's surface and thrash in an attempt to get rid of that fly or lure in its mouth.

Fish aren't the only ones that fight change. Your kids will too. When you radically alter your family's lifestyle, things are likely to get worse before they get better, depending on your children's ages. I call it the Fish-Out-of-Water Syndrome, because children behave like hooked fish, arching their backs psychologically and thrashing in the air.

You can minimize the shock by making the transition carefully and realizing what is *really* important to children.

The Power of Rituals and Routines

When kids live in chaos—wondering when or if dinner is going to be served or whether they have to find snacks for themselves, or when naps are at a different time every day—they become angry and frustrated because everything is confusing. Routine and ritual are very important in a child's life because they provide security and a sense of belonging.

If you don't think this is true, just try to remove even one activity from your child's bedtime routine, and you'll get, "But, Dad, you *always* read me a story!"

Kids thrive in an environment of safety and love, where they know what to expect.

Sande and I learned firsthand how important the nap routine was to our firstborn, Holly. One Sunday afternoon will go down in infamy in the Leman family history book. My publisher needed a family photo by the next day, and the only place still open was Sears. Holly was taking a nap. So, driven by what we thought was necessity, we woke her up. Now, here's something you have to understand. The worst job in the world—even worse than cleaning outhouses or tarring a Texas roof in August—had to be waking up Holly from a nap. From the time she was a baby, Sande and I had many an argument about whose turn it was to tap the tiny tyrant on the shoulder and get her out of bed.

We finally managed to wake her up, but it was nearly impossible to get her dressed. Nothing fit right. The label itched her, the shoes were too tight, the dress was too short, the next dress was too long. After forcing her to stay in the clothes we'd dressed her in, we took her, literally screaming and thrashing, to the mall. Realizing we didn't have time to feed her lunch because we were in too much of a rush, Sande handed her a banana . . . which she promptly smashed into Sande's face! So as Sande raced back inside the house to repair her makeup, I took Attila the Hun to the car and fastened her in her car seat, wondering what the photo would look like—red, puffy eyes and banana and all.

If I got that same call today, I'd be smarter. "Sorry," I'd tell the publisher. "We'll get it taken Monday and then overnight it to you, but it can't be there Monday."

You see, old dogs like me can learn new tricks.

You can do it! You can make the transition to a less stressful, family-oriented environment. But you have to stick to your guns, or you'll find yourself back on the wheel, running with all the other exhausted critters.

Are You Top Dog—or Is Your Child?

There's another benefit to establishing routines. They greatly lessen the probability of heated family "discussions"—a nice way to say "arguments."

Take the Leman family, for example. None of our kids have ever argued about whether they could be involved in different activities five nights a week, because they learned early on that we allow one activity per kid per semester. And they also learned early that din-nertime is family time, and we don't make many exceptions . . . especially if we feel the family has been getting too little attention.

Routines that you establish help reinforce the truth that you are not a servant to the child; you're a mom or a dad to the child. And there's a big difference between the two.

When Lauren was nine years old, our family got a cocker-span-iel puppy named Rosie. I told Lauren that she was going to be this puppy's mommy, because I knew Lauren would learn many valuable family lessons from being in that role.

Dogs have a pack mentality, and the law of the pack is this: "Friends" can be ignored, disagreed with, or even fought with, but the Alpha Dog must always be obeyed. For instance, a puppy can be wrestling its mother for fun. But when the mother growls, the puppy stops immediately and drops its head on the floor in submis-sion. What's that puppy saying? "Okay, you win."

Another puppy could growl all day long, and the puppy would just keep wrestling. But nobody messes with Momma.

Rosie had to recognize Lauren as Alpha Dog too. Otherwise Rosie would feel free to obey or disobey any command, depending on how she felt about that command.

Your child doesn't need you to be her friend. She needs you to be her parent.

For example, if the dog saw Lauren as a playmate, she'd be pulling on the leash, dragging Lauren across the street. If the dog saw Lauren as Alpha Dog, then Rosie would walk by Lauren's side.

Training puppies is similar to rearing kids. If you want to be your child's best friend, the two of you will continually disagree. Why? Because you're equals, friend to friend.

Your child doesn't need you to be her friend. She needs you to be her parent—that's her safety zone.

Like just about every puppy, Rosie had her moments of nipping. We asked a trainer how to handle this. One trick is to immediately put your fingers in the puppy's mouth and press downward on the back of her tongue until she whimpers, while you say, "No biting!" You know what that whimper is? A sign of submission. I saw a young boy work this to perfection. After days of training, he saw his dog start to nip another kid. He barked, "Out!" at his dog (a universal signal for "Stop!") and that puppy flipped over on her back and looked up at him as if to say, "I give up. What do you want me to do now?"

Sometimes moms, in particular, are rendered immobile by their kid's "whimpers" instead of acting like Alpha Dog. One mom I saw at the mall was trying to pry her son off the carousel ride, and he was doing a bit more than whimpering. But instead of acting like Alpha Dog, what did that mom do? "Honey," she said, "now we get to go to Target to look at toys!" She resorted to bribery. How is it that we parents have come to fear our child's displeasure?

You know what that mom will do next? She'll take that bratty kid to Target—to the toy section. And do you really think she'll get out of that store without buying a toy? Not on your life!

Don't be afraid of your kids. Don't let them rule over you with their tantrums at any age. Instead, realize that good training produces a whimper of submission now and then. A healthy child is not always a happy child. But children who are sometimes unhappy will learn that the world doesn't revolve around them, and they'll become balanced, contributing members of society rather than "it's all about me" tyrants.

Five Transition Tips for Saying Good-bye to "Busy"

How can you make the transition to a lifestyle that focuses on relationships instead of busyness . . . and puts you in the driver's seat as a parent? Use these five tips.

1. Don't Expect It to Happen All at Once

I fear that some people may pick up this book and say, "Oh my, Harold, have we ever missed the boat! That's gotta change *right now*. I want everyone in the family room, pronto! Now hear this, now hear this! All leaves are revoked; nobody is going anywhere. We're going to have family night every night of the week, for three hours straight. And we're going to have *fun*. Is that understood?"

If you're running for family president, good luck, because your ratings have just gone down the tube. Good for you that you want to take some concrete steps toward change. But it's better to wade into these changes slowly and deliberately, as if you're walking into a cold lake. Don't try to reinvent your family's routines overnight.

For example, let's say your kids are overcommitted to extracurricular activities. As a former dean of students, I always think in semesters; we scheduled our kids for activities a semester at a time. If you want to make changes, do it around the kitchen table toward the end of one semester as you begin thinking about the next.

You might start out by saying something like, "Crazy, isn't it? Looking back at the past two months, your dad and I have figured there were exactly four nights that we all sat around this table and had dinner together. We don't want to live that way anymore. In fact, we're not *going* to live that way anymore. We're going to make some changes for you and for us."

If your kids are prepubescent, that may be just fine with them. If they're older, however, they might look at you as if you've just sprouted two heads and horns to boot. If you decide to make changes to balance work and family and announce to your fifteen-year-old son that you're suddenly available and expect him to be home more often as well, don't kid yourself; he isn't going to do backflips in celebration. That boy will have to make some radical adjustments as he learns to relate to you and deal with his feelings about your previous emotional absence and the reality of a more intimate relationship with you. Bit by bit, however, you can begin to re-enter his world.

If you decide to pare down from four activities to one per semester, and your kids have been hooked on the pattern, there's likely to be an outcry: "It's not fair!"

"You know what?" you could tell them. "You're right. It's not fair for Dad and me to be in a total of eight activities per month. Your father works all day at the office, and I work all day at home. So we're not going to play this game any longer. You'll have to make some choices about what you're going to do next semester. You don't have to decide tonight, but we need to know in the next few weeks so we can make plans."

Your children may howl like stuck pigs.

Your children may howl like stuck pigs.

"Kids," you can say, "when you're older and you want to get involved in more activities, go for it. But for now, this is too stressful for our family. We're going to save money and effort; we're going to chill out more."

Who knows? You might even start talking to each other.

As these changes take place, you need to be the adult with a capital *A*. That is, you need to be objective and wise and recognize that what your kids may perceive as a threat is really a gift.

2. Make Sure It's All for One and One for All

I love it when farmers attend my seminars.

"You can go home," I tell them. "There's nothing new I can teach you. Nearly everything you need to know, you learned on the farm."

In a family that puts relationships first, everybody works and everybody pitches in—just as it is on the farm. This should be true whether you live in downtown Manhattan or among the wheat fields of the Midwest. Pitching in creates one of the most important gifts you can give your children: a sense of belonging.

In our culture, unfortunately, too many families live as if parents exist solely for the independent advancement of each child. When the family acts as if a child's worth depends on what he or she can do *outside* the home, children have a much weaker sense of belonging *inside* the home.

If you treat your eight-year-old like a future Olympian or a Metropolitan Opera singer in training—doing all her chores, cleaning her room, and taking care of her laundry so she can focus on her "special talent"—you may think you're giving her every advantage. But you're depriving her of the most important advantage: the sense of being a vital part of the family unit. You may end up turning that shining star into a falling star by the time she leaves home.

For a family to be a family, focused on time together and building relationships, everybody must sacrifice. And all members of a family are important: The straight-A student is no more valuable or loved than the C-student class clown. The gifted athlete isn't more important than the shy, chubby lastborn.

A child growing up in a home like that knows he may be cut

from the team, fired from his job, or kicked out of a club—but he'll always belong to the family. There will always be a place for him at the table, a bed for him to sleep on, a hug when he needs one. More important, there will always be a group of people who'll support him, love him, and encourage him.

As a sixtyish father of a late teenager now and children all the way into their thirties, I don't take this for granted. It gives me great pleasure to know that when I'm in an old folks' home, drooling on my walker and putting my underwear on backward and inside out, Holly, Krissy, Kevin II, and Hannah will be looking after their youngest sister, Lauren. Marriage may change the girls' last names (it already has changed two of their names), but they'll always be Lemans, and the Lemans will always stick together.

Always.

How do you build this sense of togetherness and belonging? By living life together; that's what defines family! That's the whole idea! If Sammy is at baseball while Susie is at ballet while Sharon is at soccer while Stevie is at Cub Scouts, you're just creating a common place to hang your clothes until you leave home the next morning.

If Sammy is at baseball while Susie is at ballet while Sharon is at soccer while Stevie is at Cub Scouts, you're just creating a common place to hang your clothes until you leave home the next morning.

Should you reward your kids for pitching in by paying them a wage in addition to their allowance? No. Dad doesn't get paid for helping when the dishes need washing, nor does Mom get a bonus for balancing the checkbook. Neither should your kids.

Taking responsibility can have its own rewards. If your twelve-year-old daughter comes home from school and remembers her job to pull dinner out of the freezer, she won't have to answer to a ravenous pack of family members that evening.

The Three Amigos, like the Three Musketeers, had it right: All for one and one for all! It's an attitude that will serve your child well for a lifetime.

3. Don't Fall Back into the Activity Trap

Once you've decided to get off the activity wheel, it takes work to *stay* off and handle the adjustments the transition brings. If you've begun putting the principles of this book into practice, you may be finding that getting the family to embrace a simpler life together is as easy as herding cats.

Busyness is as addictive as caffeine and sugar.

Take heart; the transition is never easy. Busyness is as addictive as caffeine and sugar. Teenagers, in particular, who are often quite comfortable with a frenetic pace, may have a difficult time cutting back. Even you may find it challenging to avoid slipping back into the trap if you fear your kids aren't reaching their potential. The truth is that *putting them back on the wheel of endless activities would keep them from reaching their potential.*

I know, I know—that sounds backward. Other parents may accuse you of robbing your children when you begin to pull them off the activity wheel: "What do you mean Sarah is dropping out of the traveling basketball squad? I tell you, that girl is a player! But she'll never get a college scholarship if she just bumps shoulders with those citywide rec players. She needs the competition!"

If your child is involved in too many activities, she won't reach her potential in anything. She'll lack the core value of belonging to something (the family) based on who she *is* (a beloved daughter and sister), not on what she *does* (score points, play an instrument, get top grades).

Besides, does having more options really help your child narrow down what's most important to her? By limiting your child's activities to one per term, she has to choose. Giving kids that focus encourages them to home in on their passions more effectively than trying out everything the planet has to offer.

If you're banking on higher college placement by encouraging your child to engage in all those activities, think again. To college-admissions personnel, extracurricular activities aren't all we make them out to be. "In a survey on recruiting trends conducted by the National Association for College Admission Counseling, 'work and extracurricular activities' ranked 11th in a list of factors influencing admissions decisions—far below grades, test scores, and class rank."[1]

Those who laud other benefits of extracurricular activities might cite teamwork or responsibility. Those are good reasons, I suppose, but guess what? All those traits can be developed within the family as well.

If you find yourself getting back on the activity wheel, ask yourself why. Is it because you have a "shining star" at home? Does that member of the family dominate the family's schedule? This is easy to slip into if you have a particularly gifted kid. But it's not fair to the others when a family devotes so much time and energy to one member.

The problem with a "bright light" is that it can wipe out all the little lights. Don't allow one child's gifts to eclipse the development of all the other children. (This is particularly true of firstborns, since their lights tend to shine a little brighter from the get-go, perhaps because new-in-the-trenches parents push them in that direction.)

On the other hand, you may be sneaking back onto the wheel because you like the accolades. Take Marge, for instance:

"Marge," notes a neighbor, "you homeschool all four of your kids, *and* you take them to swimming, ballet, piano, and soccer!"

"Oh, it's nothing," Marge replies. "They're my priority, after all!"

"But you've been out all day shuttling the kids from one end of town to the other."

"Well, we do put more than our share of miles on the minivan, and the kids certainly do keep me busy. But I manage."

"Marge," the neighbor says, filled with admiration, "how *do* you do it?"

As one who subtly relishes her role as martyr, Marge clearly requires a regular ego massage. But the Supermom act isn't helping her family a bit.

Let's be honest—there's an emotional payoff for a parent when others take notice. But when we're sacrificing our kids' futures to have our egos stroked, the cost is too high. When that next opportunity comes knocking—and it will—there's only one way to keep from stepping back into the activity trap.

Learn to say no.

It's not difficult; go ahead, say it: "No."

Sorry—that was a little soft. Be firmer this time: "*No!*"

There you go. That one spoken word has the remarkable ability to shut the door on whatever you're asked to participate in, lead, or give to.

Deciding to get off the activity wheel isn't a one-time decision; it's committing to a day-by-day pattern of countercultural choices that focus on the priorities of family and simple living. There will always be people who try to lasso you into their projects. While one project here or there is worth considering, the truth is that we can't do them all.

Saying no takes practice. When asked to make a commitment, many people don't have the foresight to say, "I'll think about it. Let me ask my mate," or "Let me check my schedule. I'll get back to you." That delay buys you time, provides objective distance between you and the person asking, and lets you and your spouse decide together what you can live with a few months down the road.

When you come back with your no, start your sentence with that word. "No. It sounds like a great program, and I wish I could help, but I have other commitments." The shorter you can make that response, the better. Be gentle but firm, confident that you're making wise decisions for your fam-

Saying no can be incredibly healthy for your family. That's why I call it vitamin N.

ily. Otherwise, that well-intentioned person looking for volunteers may read your hesitancy as indecision and try again to pull you in.

Saying no can be incredibly healthy for your family. That's why I call it vitamin N.

4. Make the Hard Choices

Sometimes your kids need vitamin N too. It can be tough to give it to them, especially if the idea is new to you. But if you want to shift focus to the home court, you have to make countercultural decisions that some parents blindly allow others to make for them.

Let's say your son or daughter is going to the seventh-grade formal. Other parents think it's a great idea to rent a stretch limo. I think it's an appalling idea, and I don't mind telling anyone who asks. Don't get caught up in going along with other families in a case like that.

Consider another example: Are you going to say, "Oh, I guess it's okay for my fifth-grade son to see that movie. Everyone's seeing it"? An all-you-can-eat buffet of movies isn't the healthiest thing for kids. Some films are violent; others glorify values you probably want to discourage. I'm not going to pay someone eight dollars so he can have an hour and forty-five minutes to drill into my children's heads what I'm trying to rid them of—or not introduce them to in the first place!

The earlier you develop a pattern of setting and maintaining healthy boundaries with vitamin N, the better off you'll be when your kids enter adolescence and begin taking on more responsibility. Remember, you're the parent; they're the children.

This reminds me of the parent who occasionally approaches me during a weekend seminar, complaining about her kid, who eats too much junk food.

"What junk food does he eat, ma'am?" I'll reply.

"Ice cream. He's always in the ice cream; he inhales the stuff."

"Where does he get the ice cream?"

"I buy it at the grocery store."

"So you're telling me that *you* are the one buying all the ice cream that you don't want your child to eat?"

"Uh . . . yeah."

Parent, you have to draw those lines. Don't let something as frivolous as junk food or entertainment undercut the benefits of your family life and relationships. In the case of movies, if there's one that's even close to being a risk, Sande or I will see it with our daughters, or they're not going to see it at all. We're responsible for them, and that means being there to correct a message that contradicts our family's values. (Incidentally, Focus on the Family's website PluggedIn.com, offers resources for evaluating the language, sexual content, and violence in movies.)

"You're a Leman," I tell my kids, "and we're not like everybody else."

"You're a Leman," I tell my kids, "and we're not like everybody else." There are certain things I'm not going to let them do, and they know it; they'd never say, "But Daddy, everybody's doing it."

Saying no when necessary helps get your kids off the activity wheel, even if they aren't always happy about it.

That doesn't mean you *always* say no, of course. Case in point: If an older kid—say, age fourteen—objects to going somewhere with the rest of the family, you might let her stay home. "We're going to miss you," you might say, and then go on your way. Not everybody likes the same activities; at times, common sense tells you to give your child space.

Sometimes, though, you have to make an executive decision for the family. Move gently but swiftly, even firmly. Hear out objections, because love doesn't demand its own way. But then make the call.

For instance, you may tell your fifteen-year-old that the family is going to Aunt Matilda's house for Thanksgiving. He may respond, "But I hate going to Aunt Matilda's house!"

"Honey, you can hate it all you want," you reply. "I understand. But we've been invited as a family, and we're going as a family."

"But, Dad, I'm going to be miserable all day."

"I know you'll be miserable. I understand what that's like. But going to Aunt Matilda's will be good for you; it'll make you appreciate the next day when you're not there."

At times you might attempt redirection, putting a positive spin on the outing. My doctor does that, trying to take my mind off the fact that I hate colonoscopies by making NASCAR noises as he's using the probe.

"Okay, we're in the straightaway . . . and now a hard left turn," he'll say, and then make the sound of squealing tires. That lightens the process, though the fact remains that I'm not keen on colonoscopies.

If it's clear that a visit with Aunt Matilda really is a miserable prospect to your child, just acknowledge that there are some things in life we simply don't enjoy. Neither your son's "misery" nor your empathy changes the fact that he doesn't have to enjoy the outing to join the family.

Perhaps you say to your son, "We don't ask you to do many things, but this is one trip you need to join. I know it's not fun, but it's a nonnegotiable."

Giving your kids everything they want may produce fleeting happiness. But encouraging a greater commitment to your family's values by sometimes saying no produces healthy children.

Are You Holding Your Child Too Tightly?

Ask yourself the following questions:

1. Whose needs are being met in the way I relate to my child? If *my* needs are the motivating factor, what will I do to change that?
2. Is the money I spend on my child's activities a form of smothering him or her with the things I never had?
3. Are my choices regarding my child's life leading us to a simpler, more balanced, well disciplined, family-centered lifestyle—or keeping us running on the wheel like a bunch of gerbils?

5. Keep Adjusting the Boundaries

When kids are learning to walk, you hold their hands to let them practice placing one foot in front of the other. In time, they learn the balance required to walk on their own. Then you hold their hands again to teach them safety when crossing streets. Eventually they learn to look both ways and navigate traffic themselves.

In other words, you hold them close, and then let them go.

That season-by-season, back-and-forth process of offering your comforting presence, alternated with giving your kids confident encouragement to step out into the world, marks the growth of healthy children. Your role changes not just during your transition to focus on time at home, but again and again through the years as your child prepares to one day hit the road.

When your kid is young and inexperienced, you don't just let her go and do her own thing. But as she gets older and begins discovering her own identity, you open your hands to let her take those first tentative steps in one direction or another. She'll fall down at times, and then you hold her again.

You can't keep her from getting bumps and bruises while she's trying to walk; she must learn through her failures as well as her successes. When kids ultimately leave home, you want them to be self-sufficient, to have gathered the skills needed to make it on their own, and to love others with the same love they received at home.

But how do you know if you're holding your kids *too* closely? Many adults who grew up in dysfunctional families don't know what a healthy parental presence is. They overcompensate in their attempts to break the pattern. That's why you see "hover" parents who smother their kids. But neither hovering nor showering kids with opportunities and material things will create children who learn self-sufficiency and an outward focus. Those approaches create kids who are babied, who care only about their own backsides.

Holding kids close comes easily to most moms and dads. Letting go is more difficult, especially for first-time parents. It's natural to hold that first, precious life a bit more closely than the child needs to be held; parenting is so new, and your baby seems so fragile. But as you find that ingested dirt and ladybug snacks aren't lethal and that your child has the resiliency of a rubber ball, you can begin to loosen up.

The Rocky, Rewarding Road

The transition from getting off the activity wheel into a family and home-oriented lifestyle isn't always easy, and it can be rocky. But the earlier you establish simple, family-centered routines and set yourself up as Alpha Dog, not as a "friend," the easier it will be.

Regardless of whether your child is fifteen months old or fifteen years old, there's no time like the present. So plunge on in and give it your best shot!

You'll be glad you did.

Good Question!

What practical step can you take this week to get off the activity wheel and begin the transition to a home-centered life?

How to Weather the Storms of Change

- Realize that depending on the age and personality of your kids, things will get worse before they get better when you get off the activity wheel.
- Make changes in your family's routine *slowly*.
- Treat all members of the family as important. But remember that a family adds up to more than the sum of its parts. No one family member can dominate the family's time.
- Get off the activity wheel—and don't get back on it. Don't fall for the "I'm a good parent because I do all these things for my children" myth.
- Don't expect your kids to be always happy.
- Establish and maintain healthy boundaries.
- Focus on simple living and your family relationships.
- Commit to the long haul.

ELEVEN

IT TAKES TWO, BABY!

Why a united front is always the best approach.
(With a special section for single parents)

I hate bed-and-breakfasts. They just aren't me.

After sitting as still as a choirboy on three flights and enduring two layovers watching the same looping CNN newscast at the airport, when I finally arrive in my room, all I really want is a comfortable place to rest. In a bed-and-breakfast, I'm afraid to sit on any of the furniture because, at my size, I don't want to break great-grandmother's antique rocking chair. I can live without sleeping on a pile of goose feathers. And even though I love people, I'm not keen on having lively, early morning conversations with couples from Des Moines and Anchorage.

But my antique-loving wife really likes bed-and-breakfasts. So when three of our kids were out on their own, and two of our kids were home, Sande and I decided to celebrate our anniversary at a nice bed-and-breakfast. So nice that even *I* ended up liking it. Before we left home, however, Hannah and Lauren—our two youngsters still in the nest—bombarded us with questions.

"How come we can't come?" they asked.

I thought, *I'm about to do things with your mother that would make you blush several times over.* But of course I couldn't tell my kids that.

My reply? "There are times when Mom and Dad need to be alone."

"Why?" asked Lauren.

"Honey," I told her, "I know it may be hard for you to understand, but your mom and I had a relationship before we had any of you. And this is our way of keeping that relationship close. You know how sometimes you like to go out to your favorite restaurant with just me?"

"Yeah."

"Well, your mother is the same way."

It's hard for a young kid to imagine that her parents had a relationship before she came on the scene. Lauren's history of the world began just before the Clinton administration. But because I don't want my personal life to resemble that administration, I'm determined to spend time nurturing my marriage!

Why Getting Away Is So Good— for You and Your Kids

Getting away wasn't just for me and Sande. It was for Hannah and Lauren, too—as well as my older kids, especially Krissy, who was already married and had one child of her own at that point. Remember what I said about kids always watching you? Well, even when they're married and have their own kids, they're still watching. Both Krissy and Hannah, my married daughters, will continue to watch what their parents do to make their marriage matter.

My actions communicate that, as much as I love my kids, the apple of my eye always has been and always will be my lovely bride.

These events—where I put my wife first—instill in my children the indisputable fact that marriage is important and that husbands and wives need to get away. My actions communicate that as much as I love my kids, the apple of my eye always has been and always will be my lovely bride. Sande is the woman who caught my eye before the dawn of time (in my kids' view), and she'll be the one walking by my side when my children are rearing families of their own.

This doesn't mean, of course, that going off for a romantic getaway is always easy. If you've ever left a child behind for the weekend, you probably can relate to the following experience.

The first night it's as if you're running through a field of wildflowers in soft-focus lighting. You can't believe it. The two of you eat in a restaurant where the words "kids' meal" aren't tacked onto the end of each entrée, and dinner conversation breaks the sound barrier into three-syllable words. Waiting for your food is actually part of the experience, not a breeding ground for a minivan riot.

Later that evening you have a wonderful sexual interlude without fear of Munchkin representatives from the Lollipop Guild knocking on your door or overhearing a few gasps or sighs.

The second day, your rejuvenated minds begin making the turns down that familiar carpool route.

"So, it's eleven thirty. Grandma ought to be picking Little Peanut up from preschool."

"Yeah, I wonder what he did today."

"Well, it's the beginning of Letter *T* Week. Mrs. Tibert was supposed to bring Jamie's pet tarantula this morning."

"The letter *T*, huh?" you ruminate. "That was always one of my favorite letters."

By the third day, you can't wait to get away from your getaway to hug your kids.

Spending time together—just you and your spouse—is a key facet of parenting. No, you can't always go off alone to a bed-and-breakfast, but it's good to have time alone together, even if it's just putting your kids to bed early so that the two of you can catch up.

Mike Mason, in his book *The Mystery of Marriage*, describes the demands of a marital relationship as a "big, powerful, shiny, eight-cylinder gas guzzler that has to be kept constantly on the road."[1] When the two of you are connected in heart, vision, and purpose, your home will become a stable, loving environment that provides security and a sense of belonging to your children.

When the two of you are connected in heart, vision, and purpose, your home will become a stable, loving environment that provides security and a sense of belonging to your children.

No doubt, marriage takes an incredible amount of time and energy, especially when you have one or two or a dozen nippers to keep track of. Nevertheless, it's worth giving the attention it requires. Otherwise, you'll find you and your spouse, along with the rest of the family, running faster and faster on that wheel but never connecting with each other. And when couples lose their connection, they often lose the marriage. Do you want that to be you down the road? When your kids leave home for college or an apartment of their own, don't you want to still know and have fun with your spouse? Don't you want to be able to connect over more than diapers, carpooling, and what's for dinner?

Spending time together doesn't have to be expensive. In fact, it doesn't have to cost a thing. Take a walk in a new neighborhood, talking about houses you like and don't like and dreaming about what your own might look like someday. Dust off that Scrabble box or watch a classic movie you both love.

Connecting with your spouse is about changing the pace and priorities of your life.

And one of those priorities is making sure you're putting the right person in the center of your life and heart.

Who's at the Center of Your Family Solar System?

Nicolaus Copernicus's idea was simple but revolutionary: The Sun, not the Earth, lies at the center of our solar system.

Today, no thinking person would dispute this. But at the time, Copernicus's idea rocked the world scientifically and theologically. People had assumed that everything revolved around the Earth, a view that seemed to fit the scientific data as well as the religious beliefs of the day. Humans were, of course, at the center of it all.

Many parents today live under a similar illusion. They think that believing in your child means making him the center of your family.

At first that might seem the noble and loving thing to do. After all, when that child enters your family, he's so helpless looking. He can't change his own diaper, he can't eat without you, and he's comforted only if you hold him. In short, he needs all your time and energies . . . doesn't he?

A family-centered child rather than a child-centered family produces a more giving person.

But making your child, no matter his age, the center of your family— perhaps putting your relationship with your spouse on hold for eighteen years—spells trouble.

A *family-centered child* rather than a *child-centered family* produces a more giving person. If you center everything around giving your child Disneyland, will you be rearing a child who cares about others or a child who thinks everything is about "me," and you better "gimme" anything I want?

The answer is obvious.

You want to communicate that you're there for your child. But you don't want to go too far and communicate that you're there *only* for your child.

Thankfully, God has created another institution within the family that naturally balances this out.

It's called *marriage.*

Couple Power

One of the best ways to nurture your children is to nurture your relationship with your spouse. It produces what I call "Couple Power," and it's a wonderfully stabilizing factor in your child's life. If you

One of the best ways to nurture your children is to nurture your relationship with your spouse.

don't develop and protect this pattern early on, eighteen years down the road, you'll be looking across a restaurant table trying to remember your spouse's middle name.

If you're just beginning your parenting journey, start some good habits right now. Within the first few weeks, when that little baby is still getting used to navigating a world outside the womb and its comforting amniotic fluid, leave that child alone with a trusted relative or friend for a couple of hours so that you and your spouse can have an evening alone minus diapers and spit-up.

Dr. Leman, you might be thinking, *how can you be so callous when that helpless newborn needs his parents?*

Hear me out. This excursion does three things:

1. It sends a gentle message to Little Peanut; namely, that Dad and Mom's time together is important. It says, "As much as we love you, you are not the center of the universe; everything does not revolve around you."
2. It sets a pattern of developing and maintaining Couple Power, that growing intimacy in your relationship.
3. It enables Little Peanut to sense the love between you and your spouse. When the two of you stand strong together, your child gains confidence that his home is a stable place.

The first time you leave your child behind, she'll probably freak out. The voices around her change, the chest she's up against feels different, and service may be a bit slow when she places her order for milk.

But in a couple of hours, she'll discover that her concern was a false alarm when you return to the family, stronger than ever, to love her.

If you establish a pattern of time out for Mom and Dad right from the start, two things will happen: (1) You'll be more likely to stick with it, and (2) Festus and Vanessa will accept it as part of the family routine. (Remember what we said about kids and routine? How routine gives kids a safety zone of security and a sense of belonging?) There won't be any argument when Mom and Dad get ready to head out the door.

Mom and Dad get the break they need, and they come home smiling and more able to give unconditional love and understanding to the kids.

Again, don't think your kids aren't watching. Even though your thirteen-year-old might say, "Eww, that's disgusting!" when you give your wife a real kiss instead of the perfunctory peck on the cheek, that son of yours is taking notes. *So that's how you treat the woman you love, huh? Hey, I gotta keep that in mind when I start dating.*

Intimacy: That Priceless Jewel

Take one picture-perfect marriage. Add a second job on top of the first to maintain your choice lifestyle; fold in the hope of a promotion.

For her, season liberally with commitments helping out with class projects, serving as a community leader, and maybe singing in a choir; for him, stir in coaching a soccer team that travels frequently, plus regular weekends fishing with his buddies. Add a kid or two, with three of four extracurricular activities each. Shake well.

For any family, this is a dangerous recipe for alienation, because with all that time running on the activity wheel, there's no time to stop and form family bonds.

Ask the parents in this scenario about their relationship. Ask whether they have time to go on a date. If they're honest, you're likely to get the familiar answer, "No—but if we did, I'm afraid we wouldn't have anything to talk about."

Intimacy takes time; there's no quick way to grow it.

Intimacy is a priceless jewel. It can't be purchased for any amount; it can only be given freely. To put it another way, it's like a rose. You can no more force intimacy in a relationship than you can force a rosebud to bloom. Intimacy takes time; there's no quick way to grow it. And when we begin putting activities or the pursuit of lavish lifestyles above relationships, the entire family suffers.

That's because intimacy is the foundation of your family. If your marriage goes by the wayside, your children lose the stability they depend upon, the sense of belonging they thrive on, and the sense of security they feed on.

Marital intimacy isn't built merely on grand gestures, however, such as an occasional weekend away. You also need to sprinkle in constant affirmation. Silence isn't golden to intimacy's ears. Many spouses will seek words and gestures of affection from others when they can't get them at home.

If you're too busy running the kids around and juggling responsibilities, perhaps you aren't being intentionally cruel to your spouse. But you're probably being neglectful. Some evening you'll go to bed and think to yourself, *When was the last time we even made love?*

Let me tell you the Leman rule for this: If you can't remember the last time, *it's been way too long!*

The ability to raise healthy, well-balanced children depends on your ability to support, take time for, and affirm your spouse. It's

Twenty-Four-Hour Dating

In marriage, it's the little things that really count. Here are a few tips to keep your marriage sizzling:

- Give your spouse a *real kiss*. (If your kids see it, so much the better!)
- Take five minutes and snuggle on the porch swing. (So what if dinner is five minutes late?)
- When talking to your spouse, never allow your children to interrupt.
- Bring home a single flower (pick one from the yard) or make a favorite meal "just because."
- Don't wait for a Hallmark holiday to say "I love you."
- Do something your spouse would normally do (run the kids to play practice, mow the yard) to give him or her a breather.
- Each night, tell your spouse one thing you appreciated about him or her that day.

from that strength of intimacy that your children get their security and the solid foundation that will strengthen them for a lifetime.

A Lifetime Lesson

What kind of life do you want your children to live someday, when they have their own families? Do you want your daughter to have happy, healthy children who know that she is involved in their lives? Or would you rather she be a workaholic who sees her children as extraneous details to handle in the midst of a busy schedule?

How your children act in the future in their own families starts right here, right now in your home.

Why not live the life you want your children to live?

Do you want her to slowly grow distant from her spouse, until the two of them have nothing in common anymore, and one of them finally has an affair? Or do you want their relationship to grow ever deeper and more meaningful as the years pass?

When I take Sande away from our children for a weekend, I'm giving our youngest girl a lifetime lesson: Husbands should cherish and romance their wives. And guess what? When some loser guy tries to treat her like dirt, her first thought will be, *Hey, that's not the way men are supposed to treat women! I remember how Dad took care of Mom. That's what I want.* Then she'll say to that guy, "Get out of here!"

See how it works? If you and your spouse take time for each other, you're patterning a lifetime relationship for your children in their own romantic relationships. If you have to, *make* time. That means giving something up. It means getting yourself and your family off the activity wheel so you have time for your spouse.

Keeping each other first in your heart and affection will produce rewards for everyone in the family.

My goal for all our kids is this: I hope that on the day I die, each kid will say, "Secretly I always thought Daddy loved me the best, but I also always knew he loved Mommy the most."

Especially for Single Parents

If you're a single parent, you were probably rolling your eyes at everything I just wrote in this chapter. After all, circumstances in your life have robbed you of the possibility of putting a spouse first, because you don't have one.

This is a very dangerous time for you. Why do I say that? If you're a single parent, you may be tempted to convince yourself that you must find someone to marry because you need a spouse and your child needs two parents.

But don't go there. Many single parents fall in *need* rather than *love*, and they end up going from one lousy relationship to another.

That's why I always recommend that single parents focus on raising their kids until they're of age first. Then if life is going to include marriage, you're more apt to marry for the right reasons instead of just your pressing need to find a husband or wife. If you're a single parent because of divorce, you probably regretted your choice the first time around. So why would you want to rush into another marriage?

I'm not laying down an ironclad rule here: "Absolutely do not get remarried until the last kid is out of the house." I simply offer this as a caution.

If you do choose to date, keep your kids away from the man or woman you're seeing until you're certain that the relationship is permanent (not based on feelings but on an actual proposal with a ring and a wedding date). Fight the urge to include your children in a few social situations "to see how they relate." Your kids are not guinea pigs to experiment on. Too many children are bounced around like yo-yos as their single parent dates. What does a child think about that? *I don't know what's going to happen. This week it was that guy; now, a month later, it's another guy. Nothing is safe anymore . . .*

Keep in mind that an eighteen-month relationship, followed six months later by a one-year relationship, followed nine months later by a two-year relationship may seem "stable" to an adult, but to a kid it feels like having a new parent every time he or she turns around. Adolescents, in particular, aren't going to be too thrilled with the stream of traffic going in and out your front door, or watching Mom or Dad get dumped by potential dates.

You Can Maintain a Positive Influence . . . Even If Your Ex Does Not!

Maybe you sought divorce because your ex-spouse was a negative influence on your kid. You're heartsick that the courts gave him the right to have your child on the weekends, because you know what that environment is like without your influence.

But hear me clearly on this: If the courts have decreed that your ex gets visitation rights or shared custody, there's nothing you can really do about it. If you're rearing your child with a family-oriented attitude, in spite of the difficult times and the resulting divorce, you have to trust that, in time, your child will see the difference between your home and your ex-spouse's home.

You may be tempted to bad-mouth your ex-spouse when your child returns from a weekend at his house; you may be tempted to complain about his latest arrival from the Girlfriend of the Month club; you may be tempted to use your child to spy on him ("What was your dad doing? And was *she* there?"). But if you do, you're asking for trouble in your relationship with your child.

Don't use your kid to work out your own business with your ex-spouse.

Don't use your kid to work out your own business with your ex-spouse. Your ex may indeed be a bad apple, and your daughter may feel the way you do. But your impressionable ten-year-old's mind will begin defending him, turning him into the dad she wishes she had. She wants him to be different too, but if you start to tear down her image of what she hopes he could be, she'll start propping it up with fantasies that will be difficult for you to break through. That's because, in their heart of hearts, every child wants to think the best of Mom and Dad.

Most kids figure out eventually who's involved in their lives, who shows up at their school plays, and who takes the time to listen and talk. Over the years, your son or daughter will most likely see the difference between how you live your life and how your ex-spouse lives his. Forcing the issue will only backfire.

Even though you may feel you can't give your child what she

needs, she has what's most important. She has your unconditional love and affirmation. That's where her self-worth starts and, with your help, it can build from there.

Not having both parents in the home may put a child one step behind, but it needn't keep you from succeeding in building a home and a family-centered environment if you work *together*.

Kids from one-parent homes have become great writers, founders of large companies, and even president of the United States. Just as important, many have become productive, nurturing parents who, because a single parent put the focus in the right place—her children in their growing-up years—now give that same loving focus and attention to their own growing families.

You *can* beat the odds! Your positive influence can make a world of difference in the world of your growing child. Now that's something worth working for, because that kind of a legacy keeps giving from generation to generation.

Good Question!

For married couples: How do you and your spouse make each other your first priority—over your children?

For single parents: How can you support and encourage your child without trying to be both Mom and Dad?

What's Your Pecking Order?

Take this little quiz to see whether your home is family centered—or child centered.

- The last time my spouse and I went on a date was . . .
    __ last Friday.
    __ uh, I dunno. Before we married?

- What would you do if your child wants to go somewhere, but your husband will be arriving home in ten minutes?

    __ Whiz out the door to take your child to her friend's house, hoping that you'll be home in about thirty minutes so your roast won't be overcooked.

    __ Say, "No, Daddy will be home soon. So you'll just have to wait for another day when we can plan that activity."

- Your teenager announces that he needs the family car on Friday to pick up his friends for pizza and a movie. How would you respond?

    __ Sigh as you hand over the car keys, even though your other car is in the shop, and your husband is hitching a ride with a co-worker so the two of you can go to a concert.

    __ Say, "Sorry, honey, not tonight. Your dad and I already have plans."

For single parents:

- The last time I took time for myself was . . .
    __ when I took a bubble bath—last March.
    __ two weeks ago, when I went to a movie with girlfriends.
- If you have only sixty dollars between now and when you get paid on Friday, what would you do?
    __ Buy your daughter the new designer jeans she insists she has to have, since "everybody has

them," and eat canned soup for lunch for the next five days so you can pay the electric bill.

___ Tell your daughter, "I know you want those jeans, and they're cool jeans. But they're not in the budget right now. If you really want to buy them, Mrs. Cassidy wants help getting her yard weeded, since she broke her foot. She told me she'd pay you five dollars an hour to do the job. That would go a long way toward paying for those jeans. Why don't you give her a call?"

- Your ex buys your son the latest, greatest computer game. Problem is, you don't have a computer with the right graphics card. What would you do?

  ___ Rush out to Best Buy so that your cherub will be able to immediately use his new game, since he's driving you crazy with his begging.

  ___ Call your ex and say, "That was nice of you to buy Trent that new game. But our computer won't play it. So you need to either take it back or buy him an updated graphics card. I'll leave that up to you."

TWELVE

UP WITH DOWNTIME

Creative ideas to jump-start your thinking about finding it—and using it to your best advantage.

I was busy mowing the grass when six-year-old Lauren came up to me and interrupted my backyard masterpiece.

"Dad?"

"Yes, honey?"

"I'm bored."

"You are?"

"Yeah."

"Really, *really* bored?"

"Yeah. I'm really, really, *really* bored."

"Wow. It'll be fun seeing what you decide to do to get out of that."

My daughter looked at me as if I'd just grown three noses and two more ears.

But I made my point, and even a six-year-old got it.

In my home growing up, if I ever dared to say I was bored, I'd have been handed a dust cloth or been told that there was a sinkful of dishes that could help my boredom.

So when Lauren said she was bored, I didn't "sacrifice" by leaving my mower in the middle of the yard and sprinting to the cupboard to get some paper, scissors, and glue. I just smiled and added, "Honey, you can be bored all day long if you want. When you're finished being bored, welcome back to life; it's great!"

Parent, you're not the recreational director of your family. It's not your job to make sure every moment that little Fletcher or Amber is busy and happy. If kids want to be bored, so be it! If they're bored long enough, they'll get creative and think of something to do. (But some of you might want to keep an eye on what that "something" is!)

Getting off the activity wheel will create downtime. To the busy parent, downtime may seem like the Holy Grail, but to your children it may feel like torture. After all, if they're used to you running them from activity to activity, they haven't been schooled in how to create their own fun.

You need to be very, very careful how you handle what happens after you hear the "I'm so bored" speech.

One of the chief temptations after getting off the wheel can be to replace activity *outside* the home with activity *inside* the home. Once you've stepped back and created space in your family's schedule, the question you must face is this: Will you keep time open for spontaneous family interaction, or will you rush to fill the vacuum?

Oh, boy, guess I'll have to learn how to make homemade playdough now and organize some games, since the kids are no longer in playgroup.

Mmm, I wonder if we could rearrange the entire garage so that Matthew can practice his drumming out there. . . . Maybe we'll get him a new drum set, too, to fill the gap, since he's no longer practicing with his friends two nights a week.

Stop right there. One of the best things you can do with the hours you gain from getting off the wheel is . . . *nothing!*

Yeah, you read that right.

Give Them Room to Breathe!

Life isn't meant to be lived pillar to post. If you want children who value home and family, you must allow for downtime so that your family isn't stressed at every turn. "A study by the University of Michigan quantified the downtime deficit; in the last 20 years American kids have lost about four unstructured hours a week."[1]

Opening your family's schedule—and *leaving* some of it open—gives your child time she needs to form her self-awareness and identity.

Downtime is not "free" time. When those calls come asking you to volunteer, not having anything scheduled doesn't mean you should feel guilty for turning them down. Your family needs unscheduled time; protect it as much as you would any other event.

Downtime is not "free" time.

That's true even if you don't have anything planned—other than your plan to leave room for what comes up with your family. Needs will always arise at home—help with homework, trips to the store for school supplies, conversations on why watching a certain television show isn't healthy.

Leave room and time for what's really important: developing your family relationships.

Time to Call Time Out?

Everybody needs downtime. It's not just for toddlers desperate for an afternoon rest despite their protests to the contrary. "I know it's time for downtime when Max starts to suck his thumb," said one mother of an eleven-month-old. "It doesn't necessarily mean he's sleepy; he may simply want to go in his crib and veg out."[2]

How can you tell if your child needs more downtime? Look for signs of exhaustion. If you go for a ride in the car, is she asleep before you've driven half a mile? Does he plant his face in his mashed potatoes at dinner?

Fatigue is a natural part of growing up. And kids will tire more easily as their bodies develop and they adjust to transitions at school and elsewhere. Just because your child needs to sleep more when she begins to develop physically into a young lady at age twelve doesn't mean she's lazy. It means her body needs the extra rest. But is your child's schoolwork sliding when he used to stay on top of it pretty well? Does she seem listless or talk less than she did before? Is he saying things like, "I just want to quit!"? If you hear or see signs like these, take time to evaluate whether your child may be overwhelmed.

Take a look at your child's schedule. Is it nonstop? It shouldn't be.

Take a look at your child's schedule. Is it nonstop? It shouldn't be. Some people advocate the year-round school, for example, but I'm a traditionalist who believes kids need summers off just to be kids. When I was growing up, every summer my friends and I built a raft in the creek near my house; and every summer, without fail, our raft sank. None of us ended up as an engineer (thank goodness!), but it was important for us to try. We invented games, held our own contests, and organized events in the neighborhood. The initiative we learned through those activities was invaluable.

Today's kids have their lives so scheduled and mapped out for them, with scarcely an afternoon or evening off, that many have lost the ability to get outside and build a raft or create a "pie" out of pine needles, dandelions, and mud. That's sad, because that's an infinitely important part of being a child.

The way to get off the activity wheel and gain your child's creativity in the simple things again is to insist on a schedule where these activities become possible.

When you schedule downtime, your kids may whine and complain and lie around for a few days. But eventually—if you monitor the video games, computer time, and television—they'll rediscover the glory of being kids with an empty day in front of them.

What's better than a day of kicking through fall leaves? Or building a leaf fort with plastic deck chairs? Or finding enough tall sticks to make a teepee in the backyard? Or finding a toad under the front steps of your house?

Those are the things childhood should be made of, not ceaseless "programs" that dull creativity and try to force all children into a one-size-fits-all box.

Better Than a DVD

"But won't downtime lead to vegetating?" you might ask. "Don't kids need the stimulation they get from activities and games and DVDs and TV?" You might be surprised at the answer.

One mom fondly remembers the many times she awakened with her eighteen-month-old son sitting on top of her, using her body as a highway for his Hot Wheels cars. He had an entire house to play in, but the one road he thought would be *really* fun to drive on was the one leading, quite literally, to his mother's heart!

Many parents buy all sorts of games for their kids in an attempt to stimulate their development. But if you watch your baby closely, her eyes ultimately follow you as you move from one place in the kitchen to the next. Your child knows your voice; she's tuned in to *you*. A baby's security comes from bonding with her parents—from knowing that her parents love her and will respond to her needs. *You* are the one who stimulates your child the most.

The best thing for your young child, more than educational toys or videos, is a relaxed atmosphere in which you talk and sing to him, hold him, and read those cloth books (the ones that double as hors d'oeuvres for babies) as you point at the pictures of the colored balloons and the man and the cow.

Any baby will take a walking, breathing, active mommy or daddy (or even better, both) over any toy ever invented.

This is one area in which I honestly believe that parents with less money have an advantage. Because they can't afford computer programs, expensive games and mobiles, or cable television, they may feel their children are deprived. But any baby will take a walking, breathing, active mommy or daddy (or even better, both) over any toy ever invented.

The *worst* trade you could make would be to remove both parents from the home and send them to work so that Junior or Missy could have a few more toys. The best stimulation is, and always will be, *you*.

"Mom, There's Nothing to Do!"

Does being your child's primary stimulus mean you're supposed to serve as a 24-7 activity coordinator? No. You aren't the *only* stimulation. Sometimes you even need to let kids grow through boredom.

I remember growing that way when I was five years old. I sprawled on my bed, "doin' nuthin'." I suppose I could have been outside playing, helping Mom in the kitchen, or doing a whole host of other things. But I was bored in that midsummer's way, as only a child caught between the thrill of school's end and the anticipation of school's beginning can be.

As I lay there, I heard a faint buzzing—barely audible—far away. I remained motionless as the buzz grew in volume, slowly, like a mosquito gathering up courage. As it grew louder, I recognized it as a small, single-engine airplane flying across the sky. Somehow that sound captivated my imagination so much that those minutes hang in my memory like a cherished photo.

In my book *What Your Childhood Memories Say About You*, I've written about how some of our earliest memories provide clues to who we are: our loves, our dislikes, our personalities. Back then I must have had inklings of how nice it would be to travel. The buzz of that airplane's engine must have triggered something in me that carried me beyond the four walls of my bedroom.

When I was a kid, my family didn't travel much. We took two vacations—one lasted a week, and one lasted a weekend—and both were visits to the same lake in western New York, where my family still vacations to this day. However, the sound of the airplane was part of me all along: a sense of adventure, the desire to see new places and meet new people.

Boredom isn't intrinsically bad. It's not a monster to fend off with an arsenal of CDs, DVDs, and Xbox video games. Give your schedule a little room to breathe, and boredom will move in like a fog—with potentially helpful results.

Boredom puts kids in touch with reality. It lets them know that the world usually isn't a three-ring circus all primed up to entertain them.

Remember Lauren, who was so bored? To this day, she's probably the most independent of our kids, content to amuse herself.

Your job as a parent is never to entertain your children. You can't satisfy a child's appetite for the latest, most amusing activities, anyway. Yet because

Bored is not a four-letter word.

many moms and dads today are uncomfortable with "dead air," they feel the need to fill that void with something—*anything*. But as soon as you do, you willingly put yourself and your family right back on that activity wheel.

Bored is not a four-letter word. Crucial development happens in that "bored" void for both child and adult. That silence allows us to get in touch with what's going on inside ourselves: our search for meaning, identity, and answers to unresolved questions; our frustrations; our pains; and our future direction. By taking the time to sit in silence, pondering questions and facing doubts and fears, we grow emotionally and spiritually.

That downtime allows kids time to sort things out, to process life around them. They can contemplate a sunbeam coming through a window and the dust that dances on the air, wonder about the natural world, and consider deeper questions, such as "What am I good at?" "What will I be when I grow up?" or "Will I ever get married?"

The dream sparked by my boredom that midsummer day when I was five—the dream of traveling—came true. Now I frequently find myself on planes or driving along freeways in rented cars as I head to or from speaking engagements at conferences. I don't dread that time alone; on the contrary, I love it because it gives me a chance to think. At home I relish days when I can just bum around, puttering away at the little items on my list because an empty day is stretching out before me. Relaxed days are a rare treat, and I cherish them as gifts.

You should too.

Making Something from Nothing

"In our efforts to produce Renaissance children who are competitive in all areas," said Dr. Diane Ehrensaft, a developmental and clinical psychologist and a professor at the Wright Institute in Berkeley, "we squelch creativity."[3] Ironic, isn't it, that the very parents who push their children to succeed may be failing in one of the areas that matters most—creativity?

To grow in creativity, your family needs downtime. You must practice the fine (and often boring) art of sitting with nothing.

Creativity, after all, is the art of making something from thin air. Whether it's an empty page or a blank canvas, nothing—that favorite haunt of boredom—is the beginning of any creative endeavor.

Kids need time to reach that stretching point of boredom, and then wrestle with creativity. Watching a movie or playing Nintendo may touch the imagination, but that's not the same as *creating* something from the imagination. Someday your child will be

Creativity, after all, is the art of making something from thin air.

drafting a business plan from scratch, planning new curriculum for the classroom, or working on a television show, as my son, Kevin II, is doing. Letting kids press through their boredom into something they can get excited about is good training.

What will your child do with his or her free time? Preschoolers may use a pile of blankets and chairs to build tunnels; pubescent kids may set up lemonade stands, organize neighborhood carnivals, publish a newspaper, or stage plays for parents and friends. Give your child a pile of scrap wood to build a fort in the backyard, the ingredients to make chocolate-chip cookies, or, if she's old enough, a video camera to go outside and make her own movie.

Creativity can be a messy prospect. One young boy who was heard yelling instructions across the yard to his friend who held a garden hose. "No, not like that!" the boy shouted. "You have to get wet first and *then* roll in the dirt!" Only a kid would come up with the best recipe for getting mud to stick to clothes.

When I grew up, that kind of play with buddies was an essential part of life. We didn't have great equipment—we wrapped baseballs in electrical tape, for Pete's sake. We produced plays, formed a circus, and ran track-and-field games. We even organized a league for kids on our street to play baseball against kids on a neighboring street. It lasted only two games over the course of a week, but the point was that *we* created something.

Children don't always need regimented activities. They need unstructured time, downtime—with the TV off, joining Dad and Mom to read a book or work on a project together.

Kids need time to be creative. As Leonardo Da Vinci said, "Men of genius do most when they work least."

You tell 'em, Leo!

Independence: Going It Alone

At age ten, I had my own commercial garden where I grew fruits and veggies, and then sold them at a street stand to make a few extra cents. Red raspberries were sixty cents per quart; my homegrown tomatoes were a mere fifty cents per quart!

I must confess that my produce wasn't *all* the result of my own hard work. On the grounds of a local institution, I did find some currant bushes that no one picked. Every year the currants withered and were eaten by birds, so I made the logical business move of a ten-year-old and added them to my inventory. Needless to say, I had pretty low overhead in the currant market.

The time I spent building my "business" helped me develop self-sufficiency and business skills that I benefit from today. When one of my books is released, I get more enjoyment from thinking about how to market it than I do from any other aspect of the process. The best-written book in the world won't mean much if nobody reads it; and how will anybody think to read it if somebody doesn't tell people about it?

My parents gave me a fair amount of leeway, perhaps more than many who live in the city or suburbs would give their kids today. My mother liked to tell the story of how she would wake up and find the note I'd written to her before I left for the woods, sometimes even before sunrise.

Don't worry. I've gone to the creek and I'll be back before school.

P.S. I'm dressed warmly.

Living in a rural town without the dazzle of city life probably helped me grow in independence. That isn't to say that if you reside in Chicago, you should pack up and move to Leech, Arkansas. But the bigger your city, the more opportunities you'll find for organized activities—which you may have to resist in order to give your child the downtime that develops self-sufficiency.

I know that today, in many of the places we live, that kind of broad freedom is neither possible nor safe. But by trusting your child with time to explore, play, and create within the boundaries of his or her world, you communicate, "I believe in you; I know you can handle this situation."

Make Time Together Significant!

"What's cookin' tonight?" I often asked Hannah when she was a teenager.

That question was part of an ongoing conversation Sande and I had with Hannah regarding her weekend plans with friends.

"Dad," she'd reply, "it's only seven. We don't even make plans until nine."

She was right. Sometimes they didn't.

 What All Families Need

- Downtime.
- Unhurried time with each other.
- A day off each week to regroup.

"Why don't you have your friends over? We'll get some pizzas, and you can go in the Jacuzzi," I'd suggest.

"No," she'd say. "I don't think we'll do that."

By nine o'clock that evening, though, our living room was full of kids. And they were all eating pizza and getting ready to go in the Jacuzzi.

We loved having Hannah's friends around. They were all great kids. And Sande and I were thankful they were right there, in our living room, and not hanging around elsewhere. The truth is, I'd rather have my living room packed with noisy teenagers (it often sounds like the monkey cage at the local zoo) than have a chronically quiet home and my children out with their friends.

Who cares if we could see a trail of chocolate-chip-cookie crumbs all the way to the front door, and if the couch now bears a pizza stain? If home and family are first, that means your child should spend a lot of time around your place, whether she's by herself or with dozens of friends.

Ten Ideas for Keeping Hearts at Home

How can you get your kids to stay on their home turf? Following are ten practical pointers.

1. Party at Home Sweet Home

For Lauren's eleventh birthday party, we didn't go to that Cheese-Breath Rodent place. We had a Saturday pool party at our house.

A lot of parents today don't want their children's parties at home. They don't want to organize and set up the event, and they certainly don't want to deal with chocolate cake mashed into the Berber carpet.

But the truth is that even though you may be wiping fingerprints off the wallpaper for a few days after that party, you'll remember the fun much longer—along with other times you spent together as a family, the ups and downs of life, the sacrifices you made, the joys you shared.

And when that Cheese-Breath Rodent pizza place has turned into a car wash or a Dollar Store ten years down the line, your home will be a place your kid loves to return to. Each room will be filled with more memories than he or she could ever recount.

What do you want your kids to remember about growing up?

When Lauren remembers her birthdays, I want our home to be part of those memories. I want all of our kids' homing instincts to be strong, so that when they're grown up, they return time and time again for more love, time, and attention.

Home is the primary place where life happens.

That's because, in my view, *home is the primary place where life happens.*

2. Make Home a Place of Refuge

Lauren was sitting beside me as I watched a *CNN Headline News* story about a man who was on the FBI's Most Wanted list for brutalizing people.

"Can we watch something else?" peeped Lauren, who has the disposition of a butterfly.

Realizing that what she was hearing was a little too much for her eleven-year-old ears, I changed the channel. She started to cry and buried her head in my chest.

"What's wrong?" I asked.

"Daddy, I'm afraid," she said. "I'm afraid to fly."

Lauren and Hannah were only weeks away from flying to California to visit their brother for the weekend. She feared something might happen along the way.

You, parent, are your child's psychological blankie. To build in that sense of safety, you must take time out to comfort your child as best you know how—even if you don't know the right words to say.

In such situations, defining a younger child's world for her can help. For many eleven-year-olds, that world consists of family, school, church, the few friends they have, and their pet.

So I went through the list. "Mommy and Daddy are fine," I said. "Your brother's fine. Your sisters are fine, and our home here is safe." We talked again about how there *are* people who might try to hurt others, but our family was safely around her.

Children need the sense of security and stability that comes from knowing that Dad and Mom have a plan. "That's why we don't simply drop you off and let you wander around Tucson or the mall by yourself," I told Lauren. "Do you think that Daddy would ever give permission for you to get on that airplane if I didn't think it was safe?" I asked.

"No," she replied. "But it frightens me, Daddy, that Saddam Hussein is going to come here and hurt us."

She was putting together bits and pieces she'd heard on the news. When she heard about the U.S. attack on Baghdad, and Saddam Hussein being on the move every few hours prior to his capture, and car bombs in Israel, it all got blurred together in her mind.

When you take time to sit with your child, help define her world, and demonstrate that you're there to make home a safe place, that comfort makes home the safest place for her to be.

3. Be Spontaneous

I'm a lastborn. I'm into fun! I've never been much of a scheduler either. (I leave that up to my firstborn wife and my assistant, Debbie.) That was evident when the producer of one of my shows asked me recently about my "long-range plans" for the program.

"I don't have any long-range plans," I told him. "If the show's working, let's keep on doing it. If it's not, let's think about doing something else or dropping it."

It's not that I'm *against* scheduling; I just believe that sometimes the most effective connections happen when people take things as they come.

Have you ever had a party turn out wonderfully well? Everyone had such a great time that someone says, "Hey, let's do this again next month." So you make plans, invite the same people over . . . and it's ho-hum at best. You can rarely re-create those special moments, even with the same people in the same place. More often than not, they just happen.

Create an environment for spontaneity to happen.

The same is often true with family fun. If you designate a specific night for getting wild and crazy, it can sometimes have the same effect as asking someone to explain a joke's punch line. All the life goes out of it, like a deflated balloon. Life is too spontaneous for a scheduled weekly fun night to work in most homes.

But when you keep your activities to a minimum, you create an environment for spontaneity to happen. That's when home life becomes a wonder. On the spur of the moment, one of the kids will say, "Hey, let's pop some popcorn!"

You say, "What a great idea! Turn off the stupid TV right now, and let's make an evening of it."

Then someone wonders what it would be like to watch the corn pop without a lid. So you put the popper in the middle of the living room on a sheet, take the top off, and let that popcorn fly.

You didn't plan it, but you've lived through an experience that will likely be remembered and talked about for years to come.

And it cost you less than renting a video!

4. Make It a Team Sport

When our kids were little, we played a game called Huggy Harry. I'd turn out the lights, and they'd hide in the house. Then I'd walk down the hallway with a light held under my face so that I looked a little eerie. The kids would make a sound from the rooms they were in, and I'd have to find out where they were. They loved it and screamed with delight.

One of the benefits of escaping the activity wheel is focusing on family events rather than individual ones. Dr. Nick Stinnett, professor of human development at the University of Alabama, conducted a 25-year study, which tracked 14,000 families nationwide, and found that "the happiest families spent time playing board games and card games together."[4]

That isn't to say that Chutes and Ladders or Uno has magical bonding power. The fact that families are enjoying time together makes the difference.

When you take Brock to his soccer game, he may have fun passing the ball to Billy and swapping after-game snacks with Andy. But wouldn't you rather he have even more memories of beating Daddy at Yahtzee, landing on Mommy's railroad in Monopoly, and guessing who did what to whom in Clue with his siblings?

Of course, this will require more than dropping Jimmy off at a field. You'll actually have to clear your schedule enough to sit at the table for an hour or two, ignore the telephone, and create a memory.

Here's what's fascinating about children. They tend not to notice the time it takes for you to give them rides anywhere. It may take you thirty minutes to drop off your son for soccer practice, and by the time you pick him up, it'll be sixty minutes round-trip. But your kid will barely notice your inconvenience. However, if you sit down with him for an hour and play a game, he'll remember that for days, weeks, and even a lifetime.

Games aren't the only family activities to pursue, of course. Going camping is another possibility for special family time, with the added benefit of few distractions. *Dad is actually going to take us camping?* your children may wonder. *And Mom, who hates camping, is going along with it. Won't it be fun to see Mom in the morning with-out her makeup on and with her hair all messed up?*

Those are memories for a lifetime.

5. Live and Talk Your Beliefs

During the summer the Leman family heads back east to visit the area in western New York where I grew up. One year Hannah de-cided to work at a camp across the lake, as what they call a "dishrag."

As the summer wore on, I grew antsy over seeing so little of my daughter. Which is why, when she was getting ready to travel to a weeklong youth conference at the end of the summer, I jumped at the chance to drive her to Walmart to pick up a few things before she caught the bus.

After we stopped by the store, I drove Hannah to where the group was gathering for the bus. We had about an hour before she left. We talked, and I prayed for safety for her trip and held her hand.

You might call that "family devotions."

I would.

To me, family devotions have always been the devotion I show my family. When you show you're devoted to your kids, they'll be drawn to you and your life—including your faith.

Every family's approach to living and talking their faith is dif-ferent, though. Take the way my mom did it, for instance. When I was a little boy, every morning before school, my mother put her arms around me and sang a little song as I went out the door. My friends Moonhead Dietsch and Jamie Huber would watch and roll their eyes.

"Guide and direct us just for today," she would sing, "help us, dear Father, all through the day."

God love her, she tried. But if I hear that song one more time, I'm going to hurl.

That's why, when it came time to rear my own kids, I believed firmly that the best way to encourage them to follow my faith and values was talking with them as opportunities arise, slipping them what I call "commercial announcements."

If you want a shot at passing on your spiritual and moral values to your kids, live your life genuinely and talk about your faith openly and honestly.

6. Togetherness—It's What's for Dinner

The day is always better for me if I walk into the house and smell dinner cooking—not only because the fragrance starts me salivating, but because prime family time at the Leman home has always been around the dinner table. Why? Because that's the time all of us Lemans come together and share the day's ups and downs with each other.

What are your family dinners at home like? Are they hit-and-run, five-minute affairs, so you can get on to the next activity? Do you all eat in silence because you don't know what to say? Do you eat separately—a kind of drive-through fast-food service, but at home? Are you among the 33 percent of families that say one parent's late work schedule gets in the way of eating dinner together?[5] Or is dinner a time of relaxing and connecting? Do your kids want to linger at the table for more family time?

Did you know that there are even more reasons to have a family dinnertime? There's a strong correlation between "regular family meals and success in school, better psychological adjustment, lower rates of alcohol and drug use and reduced chances of early sexual behavior," as revealed in a national study of American teens.[6]

In many homes, kids wolf down dinner, say, "Can I be excused?" (if they're respectful, at least), and then run to do their homework, to text their friends, to surf the web, or to curl up in front of the TV.

That makes for lots of lost opportunities.

I'll never forget my father telling stories at the dinner table. Half the time he'd start laughing before he even got started. Before *we* knew what he was talking about, we'd start laughing too. I'm sure he embellished a few of the tales, but boy they were funny. For instance, he and his friends would take a can full of oil into a movie theater and pour the stuff down the aisle's rubber mat. Then they'd raise a ruckus in the hope that the manager would come running into the theater—and slip on the oil! (Mmm, and my parents wonder where I got all my antics as a kid. Like father, like son?)

Kids love stories, especially about when you were little.

Kids love stories, especially about when you were little. From day one we've done what I call the "Family Fun Confession" around the dinner table. Part of it is telling stories about my life that demonstrate to my kids that the challenges and failures they face are the same ones I faced growing up.

If you know something is a struggle for your kids, talk about it on the sly in a story without moralizing. You don't want to give them a week straight of daddy failure stories, but you might sneak one in now and then. Look for their reaction as you talk. "You did *that*, Daddy? You got in trouble for that? You didn't make the team? You got busted?"

Sure, your halo might show a little tarnish, but you're also revealing yourself as real to those who matter most in your life.

Next time you sit down to dinner, share more than food with your kids. Share your imperfect self with them too. That will go a long way when they, themselves, fail at something . . . as we all do.

7. *Value Extended Family*

I spoke with one woman who said that her grandmother was "always a birthday card and a twenty-dollar bill at Christmas."

How sad. Even if miles separate the kids from their grandparents, which is often the case today, it's too bad that grandchild didn't try to make the best of the situation by tapping into her grandmother's world.

All too soon, grandmas are gone. The child who didn't know Grandma won't know anything about the lady's history, where the family came from, or what his own roots are.

It's hard to feel a sense of belonging when you have no idea who you belong to. And older people have a rich sense of history to share, as well as fascinating life experiences that can be far more entertaining than the latest Toys"R"Us shopping spree.

My advice to young families is to live near one set of parents. That means prioritizing your life around people, not things. Long-distance relationships tend to lose intimacy. You may do your best to keep up through e-mailed digital photos, audio or video recordings shipped back and forth, letters, phone calls, and visits. Those all help, but they aren't the same as living in the same community.

It's a tough reality that many of us today don't live in our parents' time zones.

My mother was closer to our children than to her other grandchildren simply because she lived in our town. And now that she's in heaven, we all miss her dearly.

As much as we might like to say it's possible to make up the difference when we give up regular, face-to-face, personal contact, that simply isn't possible. If you want the full benefit of your extended family in raising your children, living near each other is essential.

Extended family can be such an integral part of your children's lives. My kids remember the songs Grandma sang to them (yes, even the one I hated about school). My son, Kevin II, remembers how when he wanted to join in the painting at his grandparents' house, Grandma let him "paint" her wall with water while the grown-ups painted the rest of the house. Having relatives nearby gives your children a foundation of memories—all indelible imprints like yours that bind them to family.

8. Chip in Creatively

How many kids see the electric bill on the counter and pay any attention to it? One way to help kids feel they're part of the family is to make them partly accountable for the bottom line on utility bills every month.

On the surface that doesn't sound the least bit exciting. But I'd approach it this way. You might say during dinner one night, "You know, I've been thinking. This family needs to have more fun. This family needs more pizza, more movies, and more trips to the bowling alley." Tap into whatever interests the family has; no kid is going to take issue with that.

"We'll collect whatever you all can save on these bills month by month over what we spent last year and put that money in a pot. Then we'll blow the whole wad on bowling, pizza, and family movies—whatever."

That's a fun and practical alternative to barking out, "Hey, what's the front door doing open? What do you think we're doing, heating the neighborhood?" Or "Who left the lights on in the family room—again?"

Have a good time as a family charting the history of how many kilowatts you used last year and what you spent. Many bills come with such comparisons graphed out; if not, have your kids graph these out themselves. As they assume responsibility for use of electricity, gas, and water, they'll feel they're part of the action—and part of the family. (And you'll save more money than you can imagine too.)

You don't get kids to feel they belong by stopping outside activities and declaring, "Okay, now we all belong to each other! We're just going to love, love, love!" If you take that method, it won't be long until your kids are killing each other.

Five Ways to Make Home Memories

- Make home movies and watch them.
- Wash the cars together on a hot summer day.
- Have a Surprise Meal Night each week. Keep it simple (grilled cheese and "walking tacos" make most kids happy). Spread a picnic cloth in your living room for extra fun.
- Decide spontaneously on a theme for a family night: Tell a Joke Night, Wear a Hat Night, Mess-Hall Night. Give everyone five minutes to don their costumes or think of something fun to contribute. For example, for Mess-Hall Night, you could all eat soup out of cooking pots, using big spoons. There's nothing funnier than seeing Mom or Dad drool soup down their shirts when they try to eat with wooden spoons. Laughter truly *is* good medicine for a family.
- Set aside an hour and play a board game. Pictionary or other such games are guaranteed entertainment for families with children of any age.

Instead, let them be part of the vacation-planning process. Or if Dad spends seven dollars every Friday to have his car washed, give the kids the opportunity to do it themselves. That seven dollars can go toward much more important expenditures—Canadian bacon and pineapple pizza, to name one.

9. Try "Stay at Home with Your Kids" Day

Do you know what your kids are doing after school, on the Internet, or alone in their rooms? If not, it may be due to "cocooning." Dad comes home from work, and after dinner he plants himself in front of *Monday Night Football*. The kids slip into their rooms and go online or play video games.

In too many homes, parents and kids live in separate cocoons. It shouldn't be that way in a home-court family. If you want to enter your child's world, try "Stay at Home with Your Kids" Day.

You're probably familiar with Take Your Child to Work Day. I've done that kind of thing, pulling my kids out of school to visit the radio studio or taking them with me on a business trip over a weekend. It gives us an opportunity to focus on each other and talk about life and lets them see exactly what I do. It's a great idea; whether you're a stuntman or a librarian, your kids will love the adventure.

But it's just as important—if not more—to get into your kid's world. Do you know what TV shows your daughter watches when she comes home from school? Do you know where your son takes the dog after he drops his books on his bed? If you work outside the home, you may have no idea.

To combat this, try taking a personal day off work and stay at home with your kid. Tune in to what he or she is doing.

If you can't get a personal day, see if you can put in extra hours at work for a week or two. Then take half a day off and come home before your school-aged child gets there. Or schedule it on a Saturday.

Why? Because the day will come, sooner than you can imagine, when you'll be waving good-bye to your child as he or she enters adulthood. Tears will be streaming down your face, and you'll be thinking, *Where did the time go?*

On that day, if someone offered to take you back in time to spend an entire day with your kid when she was three or eight or sixteen, you'd do it in a heartbeat—even if it cost you a thousand dollars. Do it now, when all it will cost you is a day off work.

If you have more than one child, you might spend time with one in the morning and another in the afternoon. However many kids you have, I recommend spending time with them one-on-one. If you have a houseful of kids, you'll need to arrange a few of these days.

Plan an activity, preferably at home, that your kids would love. Play her favorite board game; work on that model he's building; play catch in the backyard; learn the secrets of his favorite video game; go to her favorite websites.

If you don't know what to do, let your kid assume the role of teacher. Say something like, "You know, it's funny. I really have no idea what you do when you come home from school. Would you show me how you get your friends online to chat?"

Another option is to take a day trip. Pack a surprise lunch for each other. Talk about your lives. Choose an activity that allows you to converse—not a movie. Pull out an old photo album. As you look at those pictures, talk about what your feelings were about life at that point, what you loved and feared.

You may be opening the door for teachable moments—like the time Lauren and I were listening to a country radio station. The DJ said, "Forty-five percent of single men say they have done this on vacation. What is it?" People called in with various answers, but the answer was "Have a one-night stand."

Lauren looked over at me and asked innocently, "What's a one-night stand?"

My explanation gave us the opportunity to talk about the sanctity of marriage, the reality of sexually transmitted diseases, and the strength of her own parents' marriage—topics neither of us had any way of knowing would come up.

10. Spread the Joy!

When you learn how much there is to gain from focusing on home and family, why not spread the good news? You don't have to go around the neighborhood announcing your decision to change your ways. Simply set an example with your own choices. Draw other kids to your home through your activities; don't wrestle them out of theirs.

Giving your son some spare lumber so that he and the kids down the street can build a tree fort behind your house, for instance, might make your home a pretty cool place to be. That will be more likely to happen, of course, if you get to know the other parents first, so they know your home is a safe place for their kids to hang out.

Don't think for a moment that others aren't watching what you do. I know one mother who was won over to homeschooling not by a lecture but when she realized that all the kids she wanted her daughter to hang around with were homeschooled. She just watched and made up her own mind.

That was also the case with an editor who stopped by our house for dinner once. He was overwhelmed by the experience. He saw our adult kids excited about seeing each other, bantering around the table. "Dr. Leman," he said, "most parents would give their right arm to have a family like this. How did you do it?"

The funny thing is, he should have known—he's worked on several of my books! But I just told him, "If you make home a meaningful, loving, and fun place while your kids are growing up, they'll want to return to it again and again and again."

Some of our neighbors, meanwhile, have wondered why we sometimes make such a scene saying good-bye to our older children: "Do you really have to act as if the *Titanic* has just sunk every time they're going away?"

"We love each other so much that it *feels* like the *Titanic* has sunk when they have to go away," I say, without apology.

I can see the envy in their eyes.

Wouldn't you like to see the same thing in *your* neighbors' eyes when they see the way your family interacts?

All it takes is deciding, once and for all, to get off the activity wheel so you can provide your children with a strong sense of belonging and a certainty that they come from a place where they were, are, and always will be deeply loved and welcome.

That will give your child the best chance of success not only now but for a lifetime.

Good Question!

How can you create downtime in your home, so that you'll be creating memories for later?

Successful-in-Life Kids Have Parents Who . . .

- Listen to them.
- Have fun with them and laugh with them.
- Discipline them and set boundaries.
- Take time for them.
- Are emotionally, physically, and mentally there for them.
- Apologize to them.
- Forgive them.
- Don't give in to things that will break down family relationships . . . ever.
- Keep failure in perspective.
- Expect the best of them.

A PARTY I'LL NEVER FORGET

*Why doing the right thing
always counts big in the long run.*

I had it all figured out. Throughout the summer I'd been listening for clues from the kids. From the snatches of conversation I'd overheard, I gathered there was going to be a big party for my sixtieth birthday.

The family hadn't said this explicitly, of course, but that only whetted my anticipation. The closest anyone came to letting any secret plans slip was Krissy, when she said to me, "You have the big 6-0 coming. We're really going to have to do *that* one up right."

We'd certainly done my brother Jack's sixtieth birthday up right. When *he* turned the big 6-0, there had been a huge party—we'd gone to Sacramento to surprise him. Our family knows how to throw a proper shindig, and my turn was just around the corner.

Or so I thought.

I love birthday parties. I love surprises. Most of all, I love the family gathering together for a good party. I was gearing up for a big one, perhaps the biggest one of all.

My birthday would fall on Labor Day, which couldn't have been more ideal for family and friends to converge over the weekend. I couldn't have planned it better if I'd scheduled the day of my own birth. I was ready for fireworks, for a Tucson parade with fire trucks and baton twirling and tuba tooting high-school marching bands. I was ready to celebrate! (Keep in mind that I was the baby of my family growing up, and lastborns love surprises.)

Labor Day morning finally came. I thought, *All right. Where's my son?* Kevin II's arrival from Burbank, California, was the only piece still left in my birthday puzzle and would confirm my suspicions.

But as every hour passed, I became more confused at the seeming lack of family activity. Morning came and went, and family members were barely out of bed. Afternoon came and went, and everyone seemed to be walking in slow motion. Evening came—but Kevin II didn't.

I couldn't help myself. I finally had to ask. "Isn't Kevin coming over today?"

"No, honey, I'm sorry. He couldn't make it. But I'm sure he'll call."

Kevin II's not coming? I thought. *Burbank is only a forty-five-minute plane ride from Tucson. He's not coming on my* birthday?

On any other day, I would have said we had a great evening with a relaxed dinner at home—finished off by a birthday cake. Sande, Holly, Hannah, and Lauren were there, along with Krissy and her husband, Dennis.

Hey, I reasoned, *when you're on the road as much as I am, it's nice to have a quiet dinner at home.* But to me, it was as gray a birthday as could be. I couldn't shake my disappointment.

Sande will tell you that I whined and complained all week about the fact that my son didn't visit. It was undoubtedly one of the longest weeks of her life.

The following Friday evening, I was told that the family was going out to dinner, but Holly was running a bit late. In fact, she was right on schedule. Following a secret plan, she was driving to the airport to pick up Jack, my brother, and my sister-in-law, who'd flown in from California. When the three of them walked into the restaurant, I knew everyone had put a good one over on me!

It only got better from there.

The next morning Jack and I were at the house when Sande called from an errand in town. "Honey," she said in that tempting, singsong tone, "why don't you come down to the Eclectic and have breakfast with me and Linda? They've got that $1.99 special."

So Jack and I drove down. As I sat in a booth with my menu, deciding on my order, a voice behind me asked, "What would you like to drink?"

"Coffee," I replied without turning around.

"*Coffee?*" he said. "That's *all* you want is *coffee?*"

Who is this brash kid talking to me like that? I thought as I spun around.

Looking up, I saw my son, Kevin II, beaming. After doing a double take, I was so elated to see him that I slammed my fist on the table and yelled. Everyone in the restaurant turned. It was as if I'd pulled the plug on every conversation.

But holey-kamoley! My son was in town! Five days late, but hey, better late than never, right?

The party came the next day, when they whisked me away to the local country club. Fifty or sixty guests were waiting: family, close friends, co-workers, and folks I'd known since I was a boy. I also received wonderful letters from friends and colleagues all over the country—Chuck Swindoll, Jim Dobson, Neil Clark Warren, Gary Smalley, and Les and Leslie Parrott. I couldn't have gathered a better bunch of people if I'd made the list myself.

In this day and age, I thought as I watched my kids interact with the guests throughout the dinner, *when kids use four-letter words with their parents and view reward as their right, Sande and I are fortunate to have kids who care so much about other people.*

Holly, the firstborn leader of the clan, got up immediately after the dinner and introduced herself to many guests. She knew some of these people hadn't seen each other in quite some time and might feel a bit uncomfortable. Watching her thoughtfully "work" the room, I kept thinking, *Look at that daughter of yours, Leman. Just like a fairy tale: "As good as she is beautiful." Could you have asked for any more?*

Many guests later remarked on how different our kids seemed from "most kids."

But what was most special to me happened at the end of the evening. Each family member stood and shared words that would have touched the heart of any husband and father.

Holly, an English teacher with a great command of the language and the compassionate heart of her mother, gave a beautiful tribute. She talked about how, now that she's older, she appreciates much more the sacrifices Sande and I made.

"He's always had a great sense of humor," said Kevin II. "But, most importantly, he modeled what a man is and what a husband is."

"I love you," said Lauren. "And you write really good books with interesting titles—although I've never read any of them."

Krissy shared about the importance of family. She told how, after I had spoken to a group of CEOs in Mexico City, I said to Sande, "Why don't we fly to Chicago and say hi to Krissy?" Changing our plane reservations, we flew to Chicago with two Mexican sombreros and serapes, which we wore to our daughter's dorm room, and surprised her.

When Sande got up and said, "He's the squashiest," I began to cry as if on cue.

But Hannah stole the show without even knowing it.

After beginning by using the same words another speaker had used a few minutes earlier, causing all of us to laugh uproariously, she turned serious. "I love my dad," she said as her voice quavered and she fumbled for words. "And I couldn't ask for a better dad."

That pretty much summed it up, but then something unexpected happened. *She* began to cry. "Oh," she said as tears streamed down her face, and she fanned them with her hand. "What's happening here?"

When she said that, looking for all the world like her mother, tears again blurred my vision.

Hannah, I thought as I answered her in my heart, *what's happening to you is life. You're sixteen years old, and you're thinking about all the wonderful times we've had together as a family. You're just beginning to think about college and about leaving home, and it's hitting you that your daddy's sixty years old already and that you're not going to have him around forever. You're also realizing on a deeper level that we've loved you just as you are, and that the love we share and the priority that we all place on family are priceless.*

Honey, the tears flowing down your cheeks come from the same place as the ones flowing down mine—from that deep, deep bond we share together. That's what's happening.

Some say you can't go home again. They mean the home you grew up in will never be quite the same place it used to be. But no relationship is static, and no past is perfectly preserved. The question is, what do you want your home to become?

You *can* go home. You *must* turn home if you want the deepening relationships that come from shared lives.

It may seem that your child will never grow up, but the truth is that life really is short. My brother, Jack, and I asked each other recently, "Of all the days we both have left in this life, how many of them will we spend doing something together? Thirty? Sixty? Ninety, if we're fortunate?" We just don't know, and neither of us is getting any younger.

Likewise, how many days do we have with our kids? Those, too, are numbered. I just want a shot at making a difference in my kids' lives while we still have days together at home.

I told my teenage daughter, Hannah, one afternoon, "You know Dad. When you leave, I'll be standing in the front yard bawling my eyes out." The *Titanic* would sink one more time as the neighbors watched!

And true to form, that's exactly what happened when Hannah headed for college. It was a show worthy of intrigue for the whole neighborhood.

Sande and I know that our Lauren's day to leave the nest won't be far behind. After all, our baby is now in high school. But even as our last child heads down our road and we're left blubbering in the driveway, we'll know this: The time, energy, care, and love we've poured into our kids' lives means that seeing them off is not the end.

The blessing of those relationships is that they'll continue to deepen as our kids head into the world—and form their own families. Krissy found her Dennis, and now they have two darling children (*my* grandchildren, of course). And Hannah and Josh have just started out their life journey together.

You know what's additionally wonderful? When you have kids whose hearts are focused on home and who value family over running on the activity wheel, they mature into the kind of adults you can be friends with the rest of your life.

So, what creates that focus on home and family?

- Love.
- Discipline.
- Positive, healthy expectations.
- The belief that *who* your kids are is more important than anything they could ever do.
- True devotion, lived out in the everyday arena of life.
- Knowing that the whole family is more important than its parts.
- Seeing two parents who are committed to love each other for a lifetime and who give their marriage top priority.
- Downtime.
- A sense of belonging.

These are the ingredients we've poured into our family. That sixtieth birthday party told me that Sande and I must have gotten something right, because what I was surrounded with that night tasted sweeter to me than that birthday cake ever could have.

When I look back at all we've invested in raising Holly, Krissy, Kevin II, Hannah, and Lauren, would I do it all over again?

In a heartbeat.

And I know you would too.

NOTES

Introduction

1. 2003 poll conducted for the Center for a New American Dream, cited in Sonja Steptoe, "Ready, Set, Relax!" *Time*, October 22, 2003, 38.

Chapter 1

1. David Elkind, *The Hurried Child* (Cambridge, MA: Da Capo Press, 2007), quoted in Carleton Kendrick, "The Hurried Child," Family Education.com, http://life.familyeducation.com/stress/extracurricular-activities/36187.html.
2. Study cited in Lisa Collier Cool, "Back to School 2001: The Overwhelmed Child," *Good Housekeeping*, August 2001, 79–82.

Chapter 2

1. William J. Bennett, *The Index of Leading Cultural Indicators: Facts and Figures on the State of American Society* (New York: Simon and Schuster, 1994), 102–103.
2. Study cited in Claudia Wallis, "The Case for Staying Home," *Time*, March 22, 2004, 52.
3. Amelia Warren Tyagi, "Why Women Have to Work," *Time*, March 22, 2004, 56.
4. George Barna, *Real Teens: A Contemporary Snapshot of Youth Culture* (Ventura, CA: Regal, 2001), 71.

Chapter 3

1. James C. Dobson, *The New Dare to Discipline* (Wheaton, IL: Tyndale House, 1992), 59.

2. David Noonan, "Stop Stressing Me," *Newsweek*, January 29, 2001, 54.

3. Mel Brooks, quoted in Sam Kashner, "Producing the Producer," *Vanity Fair*, January 2004, 105.

Chapter 5

1. Information on celebrity purchases, cited in Cesar G. Soriano, "For Babies Who Have Everything," Lifestyle, *USA Today*, January 12, 2004, www.usatoday.com/life/lifestyle/2004-01-12-baby-shower-gifts_x.htm.

Chapter 6

1. From Doug Grow, "Special School Crowns a Special King," *Star Tribune*, October 4, 2003, B1, 5.

2. *Searching for Bobby Fischer*, directed by Steven Zaillian, Paramount Pictures, 1993.

3. John Bowlby, *Separation: Anxiety and Anger*, vol. 2, *Attachment and Loss* (New York: Basic Books, 1980), 204, cited in Brenda Hunter, *Home by Choice: Raising Emotionally Secure Children in an Insecure World* (Sisters, OR: Multnomah, 1991), 41.

4. Research cited in "Routine Builds Family Health," *USA Today*, December 10, 2002, D9.

Chapter 7

1. "Opie the Birdman," episode 101, *The Andy Griffith Show*, Mayberry Enterprises, 1963.

2. "Mr. McBeevee," episode 64, *The Andy Griffith Show*, Mayberry Enterprises, 1962.

Chapter 8

1. Account taken from Robert Kurson, "Just Another Father-Son Story," *Esquire*, October 31, 2002, 160–68,

http://www.esquire.com/features/ESQ1102-NOV_PRODIGY
rev.

2. Lisa Collier Cool, "Back to School 2001: The Overwhelmed
   Child," *Good Housekeeping*, August 2001, 80.

3. James C. Dobson, *The Complete Marriage and Family Home
   Reference Guide* (Carol Stream, IL: Tyndale, 2000), Question
   #417.

4. Gwyneth Paltrow, quoted in Sylvia Krista Smith, "Gwyneth
   in Love," *Vanity Fair*, February 1, 2004, 151.

5. Gwyneth Paltrow, quoted in Donna Freydkin, "Paltrow
   Finds a New Peace," Life, *USA Today*, October 14, 2003,
   D1–2.

6. Ibid., D1.

7. Ibid., D2.

8. Marilee Jones, "Parents Get Too Aggressive on Admissions,"
   USA Today, January 6, 2003, A13.

9. Ibid.

10. Jane Gross, "Exposing the Cheat Sheet, with the Students'
    Aid," *New York Times*, November 26, 2003, A26.

11. Dr. Suniya Luthar, cited in Gross, "Exposing the Cheat
    Sheet."

12. L. Lamor Williams, "Getting a Jump on College Ways:
    Students at Arlington School Gain Discipline to Work on
    Their Own," *Star-Telegram*, April 24, 2004.

13. John Cloud and Jodie Morse, "Home Sweet School," *Time*,
    August 27, 2001, 46–54.

Chapter 9

1. Thane Peterson, "Take a Break, and the Rest Is Easy,"
   Bloomberg Businessweek, August 28, 2001, http://www
   .businessweek.com/bwdaily/dnflash/aug2001/nf20010828_
   616.htm.

2. Mark McKinnon, quoted in Ron Suskind, "Mrs. Hughes Takes Her Leave," *Esquire*, July 30, 2002, 103, http://ronsuskind.com/articles/000005.html.

3. Karen Hughes, quoted in Suskind, "Mrs. Hughes Takes Her Leave," 100.

4. George W. Bush, quoted in Suskind, 100–107, 110.

5. "Dem Bones," traditional American spiritual, public domain.

6. Mary Elizabeth Williams, "The Working Mother's Survival Guide," *Parents*, June 2003, 60.

7. Dr. Laura Schlessinger, quoted in Terence P. Jeffrey, "Stand Up If You Would Rather Be Raised by a Daycare Worker," *Human Events*, June 18, 2001, 12–13.

8. National Institute of Child Health and Human Development, Early Child Care Research Network, "Nonmaternal Care and Family Factors in Early Development: An Overview of the NICHD Study of Early Child Care," *Journal of Applied Developmental Psychology* 22, no. 5 (2001): 457–92.

9. Study cited in Anita Sethi, "The Daycare Dilemma," *Baby Talk*, November 2003, 17–18.

10. Estimate based on calculation from http://life.family education.com/calculator/stay-at-home-cost/55187.html.

11. Interview cited in Brenda Hunter, *Home by Choice: Raising Emotionally Secure Children in an Insecure World* (Sisters, OR: Multnomah, 2006), 33.

12. Hunter, *Home by Choice*, 35.

13. Ibid., 36.

14. Dr. Andrew Hudnut, quoted in Douglas Carlton Abrams, "Father Nature: The Making of a Modern Dad," *Psychology Today* (March/April 2002): 38.

15. 2000 national survey conducted by Radcliffe Public Policy Center, cited in Eve Heyn, "The Daddy Track," *Parenting*,

September 2003, 152, http://www.parenting.com/article/
the-daddy-track?page=0,1.

16. Cited in Abrams, "Father Nature," 38–47.

17. Anne Storey, cited in Abrams, "Father Nature," 44.

Chapter 10

1. Survey cited in Cindy Schweich Handler, "Be a Ready
   Parent," *Redbook*, April 2001, 182.

Chapter 11

1. Mike Mason, *The Mystery of Marriage* (Sisters, OR: Multnomah, 1985), 124.

Chapter 12

1. University of Michigan study, cited in Anna Quindlen,
   "Doing Nothing Is Something," *Newsweek*, May 13, 2002,
   76.

2. Katherine Lee, "Why Babies Need Downtime," *Parenting*,
   March 2003, 85.

3. Diane Ehrensaft, quoted in David Elkins, "The Overbooked
   Child: Are We Pushing Our Kids Too Hard?" *Psychology
   Today* (January/February 2003): 64, 66.

4. Nick Stinnett, cited in Charlotte Latvala, "8 Secrets of Happy
   Families," *Parenting*, October 2002, 105–106.

5. Cited in "Late Hours Biggest Barrier to Family Dining," *USA
   Today*, November 11, 2003, A1.

6. National study conducted in 2000, cited in Karen S. Peterson, "Extracurricular Burnout," *USA Today*, November 19,
   2002, D7.

ABOUT DR. KEVIN LEMAN

An internationally known psychologist, radio and television personality, and speaker, Dr. Kevin Leman has taught and entertained audiences worldwide with his wit and commonsense psychology.

The *New York Times* best-selling and award-winning author of *Have a New Kid by Friday, Have a New Husband by Friday, Sheet Music,* and *The Birth Order Book* has made thousands of house calls for radio and television programs, including *Fox & Friends, The View,* Fox's *The Morning Show, Today, Oprah,* CBS's *The Early Show, In the Market with Janet Parshall, Live with Regis Philbin,* CNN's *American Morning, Life Today* with James Robison, and *Focus on the Family.* Dr. Leman has served as a contributing family psychologist for *Good Morning America.*

Dr. Leman is also the founder and president of Couples of Promise, an organization designed and committed to helping couples remain happily married.

Dr. Leman's professional affiliations include the American Psychological Association, the American Federation of Television and Radio Artists, and the North American Society of Adlerian Psychology.

In 1993, he was the recipient of the Distinguished Alumnus Award of North Park University in Chicago. In 2003, he received from the University of Arizona the highest award that a university can extend to its own: the Alumni Achievement Award.

Dr. Leman attended North Park University. He received his bachelor's degree in psychology from the University of Arizona, where he later earned his master's and doctorate degrees. Originally from Williamsville, New York, he and his wife, Sande, live in Tucson, Arizona. They have five children and two grandchildren.

For information regarding speaking availability, business consultations, seminars, or our annual Couples of Promise cruise, please contact:

Dr. Kevin Leman

PO Box 35370

Tucson, Arizona 85740

Phone: 520-797-3830

Fax: 520-797-3809

www.drleman.com

Follow Dr. Leman on Facebook and Twitter

OTHER RESOURCES BY DR. KEVIN LEMAN

Books for Adults
   Have a New Kid by Friday
   Have a New Husband by Friday
   Have a New Teenager by Friday
   Have a New You by Friday
   The Birth Order Book
   Under the Sheets
   Sheet Music
   Making Children Mind Without Losing Yours
   Born to Win
   Sex Begins in the Kitchen
   7 Things He'll Never Tell You . . . But You Need to Know
   What Your Childhood Memories Say About You
   Running the Rapids
   What a Difference a Daddy Makes
   The Way of the Shepherd (written with William Pentak)
   Becoming the Parent God Wants You to Be
   Becoming a Couple of Promise
   A Chicken's Guide to Talking Turkey with Your Kids About Sex
(written with Kathy Flores Bell)
   First-Time Mom
   Step-parenting 101
   Living in a Step-family without Getting Stepped On
   The Perfect Match
   Be Your Own Shrink
   Stopping Stress Before It Stops You
   Single Parenting That Works
   Why Your Best Is Good Enough
   Smart Women Know When to Say No

Books for Children, with Kevin Leman II
   My Firstborn, There's No One Like You
   My Middle Child, There's No One Like You
   My Youngest, There's No One Like You
   My Only Child, There's No One Like You
   My Adopted Child, There's No One Like You
   My Grandchild, There's No One Like You

DVD/Video Series for Group Use
   Have a New Kid by Friday
   Making Children Mind Without Losing Yours (Christian—parenting edition)
   Making Children Mind Without Losing Yours (Mainstream—public-school-teacher edition)
   Value-Packed Parenting
   Making the Most of Marriage
   Running the Rapids
   Single Parenting That Works
   Bringing Peace and Harmony to the Blended Family

DVD/Video Series for Home Use
   Straight Talk on Parenting
   Why You Are the Way You Are
   Have a New Husband by Friday
   Have a New You by Friday

Available at 1-800-770-3830
www.drleman.com
   Follow Dr. Leman on Facebook and Twitter